KUNDALINI
Energy Beyond Faiths

Dr. Vinod Nath

First Published in March 2023

ISBN: 978-93-5628-141-7

BLUEROSE PUBLISHERS
www.BlueRoseONE.com
info@bluerosepublishers.com
+91 8882 898 898

Cover Design:
Aman Sharma

Typographic Design:
Namrata Saini

Distributed by: BlueRose, Amazon, Flipkart

CONTENTS

ACKNOWLEDGEMENTS

I have great pleasure in expressing my immense gratitude to my most respected teachers and Gurus for guiding me miraculously and blessing me during this whole project.

My Friends and Colleague Dr Kavita Arora deserve special thanks as she always stood by me through thick and thin and helped me at various stages of this book. Words fail to thank, my parents without their blessings this book could not have got a fruitful shape. My friend Amitabh Atrey and family deserve special mention for their constructive criticism and inspiration, which encouraged me to put in my best.

I show my gratitude to all those persons who in some way or the other have been a source of great help to me, especially Jyoti and Sanna. Finally I thank that invisible and motivating force who always stood by me whenever my morale dropped down and without whose faith my work could not have seen the light of day.

Dr Vinod Nath

PREFACE

This book is documented on the basis of personal experiences and interactions with various renowned intellectuals in the field of science and spirituality. Having been born and brought up in a cordial and secular environment in The Hills of Himalayas, a peculiar inclination for Indian culture and yogic sciences was spontaneously imbibed in me. Through this book, I tried to answer the basic and fundamental questions of spiritual life and Kundalini Energy. Moreover, I have a strong belief that this book would be of great help in breaking many established religious dogmas associated with Kundalini Energy.

Right from the beginning we are trained and programmed to have a specific but misleading path of spirituality, and usually we fail to understand the human body as a tool for all spiritual destinations. This book is an attempt to explain how different faiths and different schools of spiritual practices prevailing amongst human races convey only one message i.e. relation of psychological and physical form of the human body. Different spiritual practices are just for self development but now the programmed learning of the human faiths have established hatred and competitiveness amongst different races and communities.

Scientifically, we are *Homo sapiens* and if we consider factors for human evolution and our genetic makeup, then the basic principles of faiths and Kundalini should be applicable to all human beings equally. More clearly speaking, Kundalini Energy and Yogic science is not to be limited to any particular race or community or any faith. We need to establish a common methodology where we can develop a common understanding amongst all faiths for an even better understanding of our internal energy or Kundalini Energy. If we go to the ancient texts and look up the definition of 'Dharma' The emphasis is on disciplined life. Infact, Dharma helps human beings to sustain life by practicing certain human values, self-discipline and self-development while being in harmony with nature and the natural systems, moreover it's certain that spiritual practices revolve around the cycle of life and death itself. Everyone has to die and no one is immortal.

In between the cycle of life and death, each human has to realize and become aware of the phenomena happening around them at every moment and maintain calm i.e. 'sambhav' (equal state of mind), irrespective of happiness or sorrow. The fundamental quest to realize and channelise the energy at physical level (i.e. organ level, cellular level and molecular level) and astral levels in the human body shall invoke 'sambhav'. This process of achieving *sambhav* would require conscious efforts to neutralize daily stress, to achieve more and more by reinvoking awareness about the breath cycle and its rhythm of inhalation and exhalation. With every inhalation there is a life and with every exhalation there is a death. Daily stress can be decreased by prioritizing and doing programmed work.

On the basis of the cyclic phenomenon of life and death, different faiths describe and prescribe tips to improve life, fundamental benefits of leading a fruitful life and achieve a better place after death, which is called Moksha. Energy is needed for life and this energy covers the whole of the universe. Internally when associated with a human body, this energy is known as *Kundalini,* which is to be realized and given direction through proper 'Karma' to achieve the Dharma state of the human body. And hence the most crucial is to sustain the energy of the cycle of life and death in a pure manner to invoke a good human being or a Sadhaka or a Yogi.

As an irony the biggest hurdle for establishment as a good human being is the prejudice through our ideals, beliefs, faiths, different schools of thoughts and so on. These limit the capacity and energy required to think, observe and examine. Rather creates all the confusion, misery, terror, destruction and tremendous violence in the world. To holistically understand outward and in depth facts, and significance of establishing a good human being, can only be achieved by collective observation, examination and thinking. This is important to execute rapidly disintegrating and degenerating world where there is loss of sense of morality, sacredness, and disrespect amongst humans of different races resulting in violence, callous, destruction, enduring wars, terrorism, bioterrorism and use of atomic bombs despite the millions of years of evolution of man. Besides technological evolution, it is a moral responsibility to think together irrespective of thought distinction due to region (Eastern or Western) and profession (such as a surgeon, a carpenter, a laborer in the field, or a great poet). Thoughts are most crucial and impact creating which are influenced as per religion, faiths, knowledge, capacity, energy, experiences and conditioning. This is basically like having been 'programmed' like a computer, governed by emotional, social and psychological values. This is an indisputable and actual fact that everyone is caught in an individual network of thoughts!

Moreover, it is not just about different faiths but use of internal energy for the betterment of the human race but to awaken and improve Kundalini energy for physical and mental health on the enhancement of cognitive abilities.

CHAPTER 1

Yogic Practices and Guru Parampara

Everyone in their lives is seeking peace, contentment, bliss and relief from internal or external conflict(s). However, achieving this state of mind is not known to most of us and this is often termed as 'Mumukshu Bhav'. Generally, due to the absence of a learned yogi or a 'Guru' to guide, most of the people remain unaware of this. In the course of our lives we rarely meet people who influence us in a truly meaningful and powerful manner and become a driving force for our actions, thinking and our being. Especially during my spiritual journey, the question which constantly lingered in mind was to know the unknown. I think a hand holding is needed to explore such things. Besides this, there is an ongoing tussle between the mundane life and spiritual life for a common aspirant in the spiritual path. To acquire permanence and regularity in spiritual orientation as a guide or mentor in the path of spirituality is a must. There is always a sense of void before meeting a Yogi of such stature. Same was the situation with me which I realized after I met my mentor or Guru. I was also not clear about what I wanted from my Guru and what I was to learn from him. I had unusual notions about the eligibility as a disciple and the concept of GURU SHISHYA. Though I had some initial idea about the sadhna and some procedures to be followed, I was still not sure if I was moving ahead or not. Once my guru ji asked me to apply some mustard oil on his feet and during that time I realized that my Guruji was constantly staring at me for about 15-20 minutes. Slowly, I started feeling some vibrations along my spinal cord and then felt tranquilized. I must admit that it was the first grand experience and stabilization of the energy I ever felt! This was the first experience when I felt the divine presence of Guru and importance of existence of GURU SHISHYA PARAMPARA. In fact, this was the establishment of a linkage between my physical body and my conscious state which was realized only due to the grace of Guru ji. So I can very well institute the role of the Guru in the path of God as I could have the feeling of superconscious state. I was guided to have an egoless personality while seeking growth in the spiritual domain. We should not take Guru and 'Guru tatv' so lightly because in that case we shall be juxtaposing ourselves with the more awakened soul instead of learning. There should always be a tinge of fear and immense respect for Guru.

Guru is a guide, symbol of knowledge and a spiritual healer. A guru may also be defined as a mediator or probably a link to achieve the blessings, knowledge, experience of the Almighty. It is important to understand the importance of a Guru who gives hand holding, achieving spiritual goals, achieving mumukshu bhav to be nearer to almighty. However, this has to be equally reciprocated by a SHISHYA to persistently follow HIS instructions. The almighty is unimaginable, immeasurable and beyond the thinking capacity of a man who merely spends a life-time of about 60-70 years or may be some more on earth. It will be complete ignorance and stupidity to proclaim or mean that we know God. What we know is only the tip of the iceberg, therefore a simple approach like a little child who enjoys the company of all without knowing or trying to analyze each and everything is the best suitable approach. A simple nirvikalp (without any wish) egoless prayer to surrender yourself to supreme powers describes the true devotion. Although there are many schools of thought about GURU SHISHYA PARAMPARA, the basic approach remains similar. Guru and Gobind (mentor and God) are synonyms in the spiritual world as propounded by most of the practitioners because it's only Guru who guides to the state of supreme consciousness.

> *"Mukh Murshid da Kaba Kibla*
> *Main nit Namaj gujaaran hun"*
> *(Buleh Shah)*

It means the face of my mentor is in itself the most sacred and Godly place for me, watching the face of a mentor is just like watching God.

There are many procedures to achieve the conscious state of mind, *Bhakti* (prayer or devotion) being the most important. This requires a pure heart, egoless self and no ill-will against others, like believing in the virtue of *Sarvam Sukhino Bhavantu* (May all be blessed with happiness). Japa of mantra (especially Guru Mantra) accompanied by tapa (sadhna) as per the guidance of a mentor is pivotal for spiritual growth. There is one more aspect to it, there is no space to examine the validity of God's presence. In times of unavoidable circumstances or sufferings a disciple demands something better *in lieu* of the prayers and good deeds he has done. To demand something from the Almighty in the context of worldly affairs in a way belittles our *Bhakti* or *Tapasya* (devotion and meditation). It has to be pure, unconditional and free from the concept of *Aham* (Ego). It is significant that one develops self evaluation capabilities to rise above the demands of an egoistic self. Only regular yogic practices can help in achieving this goal. Meera is one of the finest examples of true devotion and selfless love for Lord Krishna. She was a disciple of Sant Ravi Das and established higher standards of *Bhakti* and true love for God.

No doubt, God is our refuge, ever present in troubles and somehow we tend to practice sadhna only in our bad phase. If God has to grant something according to your wish then it would come from the amount you have collected in your *Sat Karmas* (good deeds) and not from God's blessings. In other words, it may be stated that we should not demand anything from God for our selfish or wishful motives but be guided at all times by selfless motives, then the *Sat karmas* (good deeds) will have a proper direction towards spirituality. In fact, whatever is happening around us must be considered as wish of The

Almighty. Same has been stated in *Bhagwad Gita* that, "Whatever will happen, will happen for the best". In other words there should not be an iota of mistrust in God's doings. Unconditional love and devotion is essential for real spiritual growth. If we would love God and do his prayers for our preconceived notions, wishes and desires then it would malign the pure process of attaining God's blessings. God is not a medium through which we can fulfill our desires and ambitions but the only pure essential of our being. To summarize, God is in us, God is our strength, our faith, our hope and whatever makes us a good human being is a reflection of his presence.

Additionally, equal importance has been given to Karma yoga along with Bhakti Yoga. Karma has great significance for the fact that whatever goodness we generate from our worship and our deeds in our life should always be shared on a bigger scale transcending boundaries to ensure the growth of humanity. If one has achieved something in Bhakti yoga, then it becomes his prime duty and responsibility to help the other people to attain spiritual growth so that in turn they can also continue the process. In fact to materialise Bhakti yoga, implementation of Karma Yoga is mandatory to achieve the desired results. Lord Krishna and Arjun are a brilliant example, demonstrating Karma yoga in GURU SHISHYA PARAMPARA. Lord Krishna inspired Arjun to perform his duties in the form of Karma yoga and work for the benefits of humanity. With the motivational and constructive words of Krishna as GURU, Arjun, as his SHISHYA could realise his true purpose of life and execute what he was destined to. There are some chosen ones who develop spiritual qualities and there are some who are not aware of their own hidden qualities in terms of spirituality due to lack of a genuine Guru in their lives.

Apart from Bhagwat Geeta, epic Ramayana tells us about the ideal behavior and fundamentals of any ethical behaviour in a guru-shishya relationship. The then matter hero of this epic 'Lord Rama, followed the instructions of his Kul Guru, Rishi Vashisht to obey his parents. Such guidance is must for any civilization to grow and sustain its ethical values. Therefore, the one who embodies all virtues from his/her GURU for realisation of the potential of the human spirit achieves the motive of a sadhka. This archetype meta hero is at the foundation of most civilizations existing till now. For instance, Jesus Christ who came to live a normal human existence. His purpose was to set an example and take suffering upon his own body for the sake of his fellow humans. He sacrificed his life to spread the light of divinity among the masses. Jesus or Ishu is connected to the 'Nath Sampraday' lineage and his GURU PARAMPARA has been discussed in Nath yoga as Isa Nath. The present degeneration of spiritual thoughts is due to more oriented towards the materialistic world is largely due to the disconnect from Guru Parampara.

There are many gurus in the world. Everyone becomes a guru. Wherever you go there are nothing but gurus-so many that people have become fed up with all their conflicting teachings. Whenever a guru appears, he starts up a new sect. He has never been anybody's disciple but he claims to be everybody's guru. There are countless teachings, countless sects. It has become a way of earning a living, a business that doesn't involve any hard work.

It has been traced and observed that Yogis who attain something extraordinary as compared to ordinary people conduct some workshops and lessons to disseminate the knowledge. The duty of a learned Yogis is to contribute something towards the growth of nature, the universe and human civilization. However, the knowledge may be passed secretly to the one deserving disciple after gauging the ability of the student. Such a disciple is expected to spread the knowledge with pure heart.

Moreover, it is also true that the knowledge one gets should not be locked inside and must always be available for the welfare of the people. Additionally, in the service of God, one has to be free from ill-will, be it in *Mann* (feelings), *Karma* (deeds) and *Vachan* (speech) for others. An ill act/intention (maan, karma or vachan) must not be returned by ill act/intention to not be a part of the malicious cycle of 'karma chakra'. A sattvic person (free from all types of ill acts) can sustain the blessings of God and can help humanity grow both spiritually and worldly. Main motive in life must be to do something constructive for society, religion and the human race. Spirituality does not mean to be free from worldly affairs but indeed is the most constructive way to lay the foundation of living meaningful lives. Keeping grudges against people burns the *Braham tatva* (divinity) in our conscience which obstructs us in attaining our goal whether in life or afterlife. Rather, it is self destructive to delve into any kind of inhuman activity and a human should strive to do good for people. It has to be irrespective of whomsoever comes across and who is genuinely unhappy or suffering.

In the path of real service to mankind; positivism, faith and love lay the foundation for receiving God's blessings which are indispensable. Alternatively, it is like being alive which means that there is actually something very important expected or has been planned by God. God is the best judge and the real controller of life while continuing to be the real source of power, love, sympathy, faith, friendship and care in the human heart.

A human who has been chosen to give service to mankind is required to be guided by a GURU and there are numerous examples of GURU SHISHYA following these yogic paths for generations forming a type of lineage of gurus termed as GURU PARAMPARA. The first Guru Shishya parampara was established by Shiva and Shakti. Mother goddess asked many queries regarding awakening of spiritual energies and powers in the human body to Lord Shiva. The queries included a variety of facets of yogic sciences. In answer, Lord Shiva gave the methodologies of Vigyan Bhairav Tantra which included about 112 avdharnas or kriyas which we generally use in the present day yogic sciences. The main query was to know if there is any supreme energy which governs the Mantras and Shabd Brahma ?

Lord Shiva explained this through nine forms of Purush tatvas, which have been referred to in our Shastras. Then she asked which tatv governs all nine Purush Tatvas. In answer to this Lord Shiva, while trying to satisfy her curiosity about the moksha, gave her Guru Diksha and propounded the first idea of Guru-Shishya parampara. This later on led to the formulation of sects named Shaivism, Shaktism and Vaishnavism. With passage of time more divisions took place to lead to various branches as shown below..

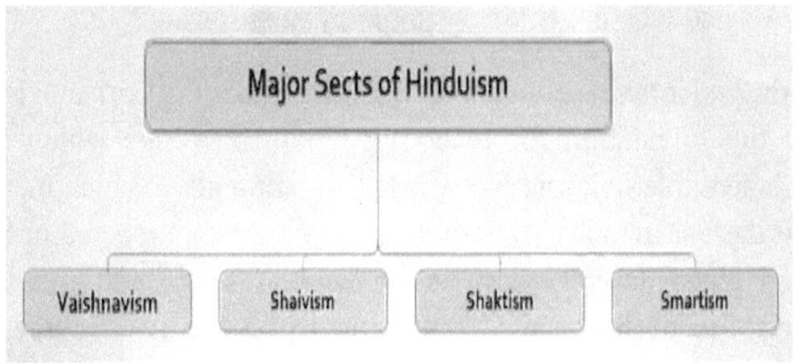

Fig. 1 Major sects of Hinduism

Great efforts were made by Adi Shankara to unite Hindus and organise different sects. He is remembered for uniting the worshippers of Ganesh, Surya, Vishnu etc. Shankaracharya also unified the Advait Vedanta schools with the Bhakti schools of Vedanta by saying that Bhakti is a very useful method to attain *'Chitt shuddhi'* (purity of soul). It is another matter that Bhakti

Vedantians did not accept his unification scheme. His establishment of 4 mathas in 4 corners of India and journey across the length and breadth of Bharat laid the foundation of united hinduism and akhara system. Here, I am trying to elaborate many facets of different schools of spiritual thoughts apart from hinduism and trying to explain how these are related to one another and their basics remain the same.

Considering the fact that all the sects originated from Shiva and Shakti Guru Parampara, the basic concept of Vishnu and Shaivism is the same. There is no division between them so that they complement each other. Shaktism on the other hand is little different but is equally essential for the smooth functioning of earthly affairs as well as Yogic paths through basic constituents Wind, Fire, Earth, Water and Aakash which are basic sources of our energy and the conscience. The instructor or GURU who always guides in doing the best and directs to uphold the light of goodness while restricting misdeeds. This concept of good karma or deeds and bad karma is very complex and needs to be understood how it regulates.

Belonging to worldly affairs, we can pay our homage to God by praying to him everyday, be it any religion. We have scriptures and holy books which not only praise our almighty but also the "Shakti" which helps to achieve the final destination of life. It is this Shakti that blesses us with great positive and constructive energy and great motivation to lead our lives sacredly and for the welfare of the people. It increases our channels of energy, empowers us to overcome our limitations and can help us to differentiate between good and evil. At the same time it makes us confident about our being and doesn't let us get bogged down by this world of selfishness. It guides to tread on the path of righteousness and virtue regulated and directed by the Almighty.

To keep a balance in our lives we must continue our '*Nitnem*' (regular prayers) to maintain this energy in our body. This energy, is a form of Guru tatv which rises with the 'shabad'. The shabda brahma is given by Guru and brings a balanced state of mind: of happiness and peace. *Nitnem increases purity*, unselfishness and unconditional love for God. It strengthens us and reminds us that feelings, emotions and faith are the foundation of devotion and worship.

The balanced state of mind achieved through our prayers is indeed a difficult task but can be attained through regular practice. Whenever an uneven thought comes to your mind while your prayers, try to avoid it by nullifying that thought. Initially varied thoughts will come to your mind but with practice one would be able to achieve the desired state of mind. Determination is another factor for the regularity of prayers. Sometimes we do not feel like offering prayers for different reasons.

Our stubbornness may deter the growth of our spiritual journey. Rather making our shortcomings the impediments of our journey we should utilize them constructively towards the attainment of our destination.There is no religion which restricts God from pouring out his blessings for man belonging to some other religion. In a nutshell, we may say that God is for all of us irrespective of our caste, creed and religion. Whichever deity we believe in, can bless a person irrespective of their religion and without any biases. Almighty is free from all the bondages of religions which have been created by the psyche of human beings only. Along with a firm belief in the Almighty's work , prayers give us the positive and constructive energy to lead our lives in a beautiful manner. Happiness and sorrow are a part of everyone's life, it is patience and will power and our firm belief in God that keeps us going, hoping always for the best.

There is one more dimension to worship, it should not be taken in a slight manner but should involve Fear along with Love, Faith and Purity. The role of fear is essential; as it always keeps a man on toes and would never let him do misdeeds. It restricts the ego to get into the mind of a disciple that he is the only one who is disciplined and a great disciple of God. Selfpraising is an act of self- immolation or suicide. The moment one does self-praising, ego enters the soul of the person and he assumes himself to be superior to the rest of the people. Practitioner starts thinking that nobody knows God better than him. It is the beginning of one's degeneration in spirituality.

If someone is especially blessed by God in terms of devotion and worship then it should be taken in the sense that God is preparing for the service of mankind, the evolution of the human race and not for making him superior to others. He chooses a few people to do so because all cannot become the same or all cannot pursue the difficult path of spirituality. Those who are little better in terms of spiritualism can be guided by the Guru to enhance their contribution towards the growth of mankind in terms of goodness and taking them out from their woes.

The treasure of God is limitless, be it knowledge, blessings or His love. A story of an old man in Sufism truly reflects it:

Once there was an old blind man who was wandering in the desert in search of water, his feet were cracked as he was barefooted. There he met a caravan, a man on the camel asked the blind man, "What are you doing in the desert?"

The old man replied I am thirsty and need water. The man asked his comrade to give him a glass of water. When the old man was drinking water the man upon the camel saw his feet. The man asked what else do you want just tell me I would give you.

The old man replied as I am a blind person I would like to see your face who has given me water. The man (Hazrat Ali) gave him eyesight. Then he asked what else do you want?

The old man replied my feet have worn out as I don't have shoes to protect them he said to his comrade to give him a pair of shoes. Then he said what else do you want? The old man replied I am tired of walking down the desert. Maybe I have a camel ? The man said to the people with him to give him all the camels. All the individuals sitting upon them ran from there, scared of God's will to give them to him. This is called the *Rehmat* (blessings of God) you never know when you come to him for a meager thing and he thinks of giving you the whole world.

God's power and limit is immeasurable so are the Yogis and the great Saints but the realisation of these powers need proper direction and bent of mind which in turn can be achieved by the grace of Murshid or Guru . The process of reaching the power of God has always triggered spiritualists on the path of *Ridhi* and *Sidhi* (attainment of spiritual power) of their idol but the very blessings of God upon one is always and will always has an edge over those *Ridhi* and *Sidhi* because nobody can do anything even after acquiring powers through *Tapa* and *Pooja* without the consent of God.

The showering of blessing by God may come upon one through the mediator or the Saints. It is the matter of destiny or the preplanned scheme of the universe to give due to the deserving. It is a true incident that was narrated to me.

An old man and his wife went for a pilgrimage while on their way to the sacred place they met a Saint who asked them, "Where have you come from?"

The old man replied from Mumbai. The Saint asked, "On what purpose have you come from Mumbai?"

The man replied to meet a Great Yogi.

The Saint asked, "Do you know the meaning of a Great Yogi?"

The man said, "Well I do not know."

The Saint replied to the person who was a realised person and had the capacity to talk to God.

The Saint asked, "What will you do after meeting a Great Yogi?"

The man replied I will talk to him.

The Saint replied that the person who has the capacity to talk to God why would he talk to you.

The old man was silent. Then the Saint enquired for what else have you come for?

To have Darshan of God.

The Saint asked do you know the meaning of Darshan.

The Saint said come along with me, the old man and his wife went after the saint, he sat under the tree and said Ohm and after sometime he asked them to keep in their heart whatever they have seen and should not disclose to anyone.

At present our traditional values and culture is taking a back seat due to modernization in our country. If a person offers or performs a prayer he is labeled as an old man living in the young world. It is our duty and immediate need to restore our tradition so that the new generation can acknowledge the fact that how privileged and blessed they are to have been born in such a pure and divine country India.

India is an epicenter of spiritual growth and attains the desired energy to channelize one's Kundalini. It is in India only that a person can achieve all the 7 chakras with the help of an able Guru. The benefit of 7 chakras not only helps to cure the deadliest diseases or disorders but it also connects us to the roots which are now long ago forgotten by our generation and civilization. India has acquired in abundance whatever is essential for the growth of our nation both monetarily and globally but it has been unsuccessful in retaining the true wealth of our country i.e. our traditional culture and the very soul of our country spiritualism.

Sometimes our life is full of struggle because of our own deeds and sometimes people make us suffer. As a result of which we demand for a just punishment for them from the Almighty. The fact is we should not ask for their karma fruit from God because if we do so God or Deity will certainly make them realise but for that even we have to pay a heavy amount in the form of decrement in our own earned pure and positive karmas. Let others pay their karmas or good karmas in the form of punishment. God is never unjust, He is very objective in his judgment, and He always waits for any human being to supersede his acquired wealth so that his misdeeds could be paid off. Therefore we should not interfere with the god's circle of justice. We should have complete faith upon God's grace and doings if we are suffering, it means God is anointing us from the sins we have committed. We should not revert back to them because in this way we shall be setting the scores, moreover we should have any revengeful sadhna. One should have a forgiving nature and there should be a feeling of love and care for everyone. One should not back bite others because in this manner we will be bringing negativity in both thoughts as well as in our Karmas.

Aspiration for knowledge beyond one's sustenance is undesirable because the knowledge about God is beyond our life span. So we must go for the knowledge as per our body and mind and not as a mere curiosity to know the complexities involved. Not everyone's body and soul is fit to acquire knowledge. It is our pure deeds of our previous birth that allows our body, mind and soul to be blessed with the best of the knowledge, Guru's teachings and blessings of God.

Meditation is of two kinds, first and prime focus should be of self development and the other one is to develop oneself as well as other people who come along with us in our journey of life. The one is done for oneself however develops our energy level and a glow on our face but the one who serves humanity is of high significance as whatever one gets it should be disseminated rather than keeping to oneself.

There are certain incidents about great sacrifices of people for GURU PARAMPARAS in different faiths across the globe. Guru and disciple relationship is of great stature and has a lot of depth and understanding. A Guru always tries to improve his disciple in one or the other way and this checking doesn't complete unless the disciple learns and acquires the required virtue for the attainment of spiritual aspects. There are so many true and authentic stories which speak of an unquestionable faith and love between them. Guru may be very tough with the disciple but it is always for improvement. It is a matter of soul. Their souls get interlinked when faith takes birth in their relationship. It is not the imparting of knowledge from mouth to ear but it is the knowledge which transmits from Master's soul to disciple's soul and the medium depends upon the tradition of the sect. The topmost thing is the trust in one's Guru.

When we unfold history we come face to face with people who actually tread on the path of their Guru and became their loved ones. It has always been a torch bearer of the pure and unique relationship of Guru and his disciples:

On April 13, 1699, Baisakhi, thousands of followers gathered on the call of the tenth Guru Gobind Singh ji to celebrate Baisakhi at Anandpur Sahib. On the day Guru Saab went into a nearby tent and came out with his bare sword in his hand, he raised his voice and said, "From you people of mine, I want a head."

The people got scared by such an order. Guru Saab again said, "Is there no one here who loves me enough?"

This time a man came forward, Daya Ram and said humbly, "O great one! I offer my head, and my fortune would be great if you accept it."

The Guru took him inside the tent, the people heard the strike of the sword and the stream of blood came from the tent. The Guru came out his sword, soaked in blood and the Guru demanded another head. After another call Dharam Das came up and offered his head. The Guru took him inside the tent and likewise the Guru demanded three more heads consecutively. This time three of his followers came up: Mohakam Chand, Himmat Rai, and Sahib Chand. The Guru looked satisfied. He took them inside the tent one by one and the people heard their fate and saw the proof streaming out. The people were terrified, some of the least brave fled. The tent was silent and the five men were thought dead. After sometime the Guru came out behind him came the five men dressed in beautiful saffron robes, with radiant faces each holding their head, the crowd petrified.

The Guru spoke gently "These are my true loved ones "The Panj Piarey" now that they are here the community need not fear."

The above narrated historical fact showcases that one who always keeps his complete faith in his Guru and doesn't doubt his intentions always becomes his and God's loved ones. Those who acquire such virtues are the ones who can actually serve God and can pave the way for others to follow the holy path to reach the final destination of our lives, the Almighty.

It is a common practice by people to believe in innumerous Gods, Saints, Idols etc. but rather than perplexing oneself into so many different things and beliefs one should opt for one God. However collectively they all are one but faith or performing rituals for so many make the things complex for the universal energy also which is to be given the direction during sadhna. As it becomes perplexing for the universe to decide who should grant you the benefits or the blessings.

Sometimes desire to get more knowledge has a negative impact on spiritual growth as gathering of just textual concepts leads to arrogance. Much knowledge and desire to get more becomes an obstacle for us in the journey. Everyone's body and sensibility is not of equal level to bear the changes in energy levels as well as the mental level. The presence of an able Guru or a Mentor is necessary for its energy channel. In the absence of Guru or Mentor when the efforts are made to achieve more then variations in body and mannerisms come, so in order to acquire a balanced state of mind and body one should not practice anything without having given a thought. God has sent us to do Karmas and Bhakti but in balance. One should not do too much either of the two without the proper guidance of an able Guru. One more important aspect of knowledge is that it must be realised one not the grabed one, this rule holds equally to both worldly and spiritual knowledge. The extent of the knowledge increases with a meditative mindset. The realised knowledge gained with internal development is mostly permanent and egoless.

Any knowledge that gives birth to self-praise and ego is of no use because the major aspect of imparting knowledge is the evolution and not the nourishment of baseless ego or superiority complex. The knowledge which helps in the development of the society and people should be imparted extensively and should also be updated from time to time to make it more effective for the welfare of the people. It is the highest form of creation. These type of knowledge can only be achieved when we follow the instructions of a Guru or mentor keeping in mind the Guru-Shishya parampara and its dignity.

We have different seasons similarly the energy levels in our body changes from time to time depending upon the various factors. On the path of spirituality our body and mind are not much in tune with the newly revealed complexities and novelties in our body and mind. Vibrations open our self and our corporeal body to a new world altogether in which we live. It begins communicating with the universe. The major thing that should be kept in mind is we are part of the universe and the energy system of the universe is related to us.

Whenever we sit for prayers sometimes we feel sleepy or drowsy however we may not feel as such before the beginning of the prayers. The reason being the prayer attracts the cosmos or the universe which in turn causes the drowsiness on part of the devotee. The more a person gets into drowsiness while praying the more prone to the first stage of Samadhi (conscious state). One can also experience such state happening listening to devotional song; we get so much connected and united with the lyrics, music, and the feel of the song that it draws us towards a trans which is the initial stage of Samadhi . Samadhi *(sam adhi)* means the balance of mind, body and soul. Synchronization is required during performing prayers. It helps in the elevation and conservation of energy levels. It could be attained more constructively through Yoga.

There is one more concept of Bhakti yoga, however it may seem quite complex but has an innate depth. One must aspire or should try to achieve root of the things rather than wandering aimlessly for example if one wants to have something in life, he should aspire for the main aim and should not dwell into other myriad world where he would get lost ultimately or may slower his process for the attainment of the main aim. Similarly in the path of Bhakti one should aim. It is very apt and just to get blessings from different sects of religion or God but at the same time it is important to be with the root the rest of the blessings or good wishes will automatically come thereon.

It should be a humane act of every individual to help the people in distress. At present money has got a supreme place in our society. But rather than making it an unending insatiable monster, one must turn or use it constructively towards the development of the people who are very much in distress. We come across so many people at our workplace, home, or the places with whom we are familiar are actually going through a very hard time. We must try to help them in the best possible manner with pure feelings, without any preconceived notion that such kind of charity is going to uplift one's Karmas etc. It should be a selfless effort on our part only then it would actually become a Karma which is equivalent to Bhakti Yoga as well as Karma Yoga.

One must not dwell into too many logics in the process of spiritualism, because it hinders the growth, too many questions makes a person too rational with answers which are resultant of lowering the level of faith. If we start pondering over how everything works etc. because when a person in the attempt to tell people that he is very knowledgeable in this context actually leads to complexity. When we get too analytical about a thing it ends up breaking or creating doubt about the things we had actually believed in.

Faith has no definition so far. It is a state where reason, knowledge and pragmatic approach becomes subservient. Faith is the virtue of dedication both emotionally and psychologically in one's Mentor, Guide, Guru, and God. It is a stick which actually helps us to retain in this world, which helps to create hope and assists us in completing the journey of our lives.

The evolution and development of a person in the context of spiritualism is not restricted to our present birth but it has its root in the previous birth of ours. What we are today finds its roots or answer in what we were then. Actually we all are in the process of evolution, an evolution which has its origin from the many previous births of ours. Some people acquire spiritual growth faster than others because they may have acquired or earned its balance in the previous birth which may be the basis of or the foundation of our acquired spiritualism since the time of our birth

The main Guru of our living beings can only be God. No other being has the ability to become a Guru. On the contrary a person can be a mediator to help acquiring the spiritual bliss and the path towards the attainment of God. The presence of a preceptor or *Murshid or Guru* in the life of a person may be a matter of chance but most of the time it has always been a matter of destiny. Certainly its not by chance. For a fortunate disciple is the result of one's pure heart, dedication and but more it has always been a matter of pure, dedicated and individual quest for his ultimate Guru. If someone is pure by heart, by actions and has a passion as well as the dedication to meet the Supreme Power, then God indeed bestows upon him the companionship of a *Murshid*. Guru is the one who not only corrects our mistakes but also has a beautiful heart to bestow his disciples the greatest of the gifts of the universe.

Gorakhnath, the greatest of all yogis, asked his teacher, Matsyendranath, the First Yogi in this creation cycle: "Who is the Primal Guru?" And Matsyendranath answered: "The Eternal Beginning less One Anadi is the Primal Guru". He continued: "Realization of that Guru gives us immortality".

When Gorakhnath asked: "Who is the Guru that leads to the Goal?"

Matsyendranath told him: "Nirvana itself is the Guru that leads to the Goal." That is, the liberated condition of the Self, though presently buried beneath the debris of lifetimes of ignorance, is itself the inspirer and guide to the revelation of our eternal liberation. The verdict and orders of the Guru is the order of God. One should never doubt the intention of one's Guru because it's like doubting the belief you are investing in. No matter how strict one's Guru is, he always wants his disciple to grow both spiritually and as a good human being because that is the ultimate responsibility of a Guru. Once Guru Matsyendra Nath asked Guru Gorakhnath ji to bring *bhiksha* (alms) from the nearby village. One lady gave Guru Gorakh Kheer (a sweet dish). When he brought all the things he received from bhiksha, Guru Matsyendra asked him to bring kheer once again from the lady he went back and asked for the kheer the lady gave him with a smile he repeatedly came to ask for the kheer on his Master's orders. The lady said I think you ate it on the way and are asking for more in the name of your Guru. Guru Gorakh said I am not lying, my Guru has asked me to bring it. The woman said how can I believe you?

Guru Gorakh took out his eye and gave it to that lady and went back. Guru Matsyendranath asked what happened to your eye? Guru Gorakh narrated the incident. Guru Matsyendranath was so happy with Guru Gorakh that he said you shall be the greatest guru from now onwards greater than me. The incident shows the complete faith in guru and his ways and on the path of spirituality nobody is free from test. One has to pass it in order to be a humble servant.

One can not free oneself from *pariksha* or examination on the path of God, when we enter our schooling we begin with training, then we take tests and then we are given our results. Similarly on the path of spirituality one cannot assume himself free from the necessity of *pariksha*. It is essentially important for the development of his spiritual growth. It is an instrument to check his development as a disciple as well as a human being in relation to God as well as his Guru.

The concept of *pooja* (worship) has got a very deep rooted meaning, it means whenever we try to invoke the blessings of God we are offering ourselves in a zero state to him. The *pooja* should not be influenced by our day today dealing with the people; it should be a selfless effort on our part to seek the blessings of ALMIGHTY.

The connection between one soul to another cannot be formed unless the feelings are very pure for each other. The relationship between the Guru and disciple is more of soul than of worldly relationship, if a disciple is able to make a pure connection with his Guru then there is no other relationship like that in this world. In other words when one has taken the right path to achieve the aim of one's life that is God.

Any service in the name of God should be free from all the desires or selfish motives of the person. If there is some hidden intention behind it then it suffers from a dosha. That is more of a transaction than a real love and care for one's Almighty or Guru.

The Guru always gives his knowledge to those people who deserve it but at the same time he makes sure that whatever he is giving to his disciple is in accordance with intellect and Karmas. No Guru distributes knowledge like charity. The ultimate desire of Saints or real Guru is the development of human beings both in values and spirit.

Humbleness *(Namarata)* makes us closer to Guru and God. Knowledge is a very pure thing and to attain it the disciple has to be very humble and after acquiring it humbler.

Once Alexander the Great saw a hermit and thought the people who are so knowledgeable have to be in my country.

He went to a sage and said, "I have come here to take you to my land."

The sage asked for what?

Alexander said, "People like you should be in my country so that you can disseminate your knowledge to my countrymen."

The sage said, "But I do not want to go with you."

Alexander said, "Do you know whom you are talking to?"

The sage replied, "Yes I know a person who is a slave to his passions."

Alexander said, "If you will not listen to me I will make you my slave and will kill you."

The sage said calmly refused the invitation.

Alexander said, "How can you say that?"

The sage replied, "Anger is my slave and you are the slave of your anger.

In this manner you are the slave of my slave"

Hearing it Alexander realized his mistake and went from there.

Fictitious behavior if part of nature may deter the process of spirituality also. True to one's actions and thoughts is one of the requisites on the path of Bhakti. If that is missing, a person cannot grow, it will always be an obstacle on the journey of a spiritual being.

Money cannot substitute *Kar sewa* (physical labour as a mark of devotion). It is because when the devotee does *sewa* in this manner he is offering his body at the altar of God. In other words it is karma yoga and may be considered equivalent to Bhakti yoga. When a person starts sharing his Karma Yoga or Bhakti Yoga with people he starts debiting his karmas account. One should never proclaim the things one does for the guru or God because at that very moment your deeds end there.

A child is always regarded as the reflection of God because he never intellectualizes a thing and is free from any dosha of any kind. His love for everyone is the same. He has absolutely no expectation from others what he looks for is love. He never doubts the intention of anyone because he has no such characteristic in him, he is pure *atma*, but when he comes in connection with worldly affairs then his vices supersedes his virtues. The approach of any disciple should be like a child that has complete faith in his Master and his ways like Drhuv and Prahalad had faith in their Gurus and with their sheer dint of devotion they were able to achieve the blessings and place in the heart of God.

Bhakta Prahlada was born to Hiranyakashipu and Kayadu, an evil king who had been granted a boon that he could not be killed by man or animal, day or night, inside or outside. Despite several warnings from his father, Prahlada continued to worship Lord Vishnu. Hiranyakashipu then decided to poison him, but Prahlada survived. Then he tried to kill the boy with elephants, but he lived. Prahlada was put in a room with venomous snakes, but all was in vain.

Holika the sister of Hiranyakashp, was given a boon that she could not be hurt by fire. Hiranyakashipu puts Prahlada on the lap of Holika when she sits on a pyre. Prahlada prayed to Lord Vishnu to help him. Holika was burnt to death and Prahlada was alive.

Hiranyakashyap, became impatient and when was about to slain Prahlada, the incarnation of Lord Vishnu Narasimha came as the half-man, half-lion for saving his bhagat's life. Hiranyakashyap was killed on the threshold at dusk. The story of Prahlada strengthens our belief that paramount faith in God saves a man from many obstacles and hurdles of life. Devotion can be practiced at any time. Age does not matter and God is Omnipresent.

The love and devotion towards the Almighty is the supreme karma or YOGA of an individual. It is the path of purity and a lot of blessings come upon the way of a disciple in the form of God's storehouse of love. The story of Dhruva epitomizes the beautiful relationship a man enjoys with god through his selfless and pure devotion towards Almighty.

There was a king called Uttanapada. He had two wives Suniti and Suruchi. Suniti had a son; Dhruva, while Suruchi's son was called Uttama. Suruchi was younger and more beautiful. The king was very much in love with Suruchi. Dhruva and Uttama were both five years old, Dhruva was neglected by his father. Dhruva made up his mind to go in search of Lord Vishnu and begged his mother to allow him to do so. Dhruva bowed to her and left for the forests. When any one seeks out God with a sincere heart, God Himself will send His messengers to help him and put him on the path. As Dhruva left the kingdom behind and was slowly walking towards the forest, Narada accosted him and asked, "Son, you are very young, barely five years. Who are you? Why are you wearing clothes made of tree bark? Come, I will take you back to your parents."

Narada was a great devotee of Lord Vishnu. He wanted to see if Dhruva was firm in his determination to do tapas for the Lord; and if he was, he would help him in doing the tapas. Dhruva did not know who Narada was. But he was brought up by his mother with morals and virtues. He bowed at the feet of the sage with great devotion and told him his full story. He concluded by saying, "I will do a lot of tapas in the forest until Lord Narayana gives me a vision and my father's love." Narada tried to dissuade but Dhruva was very firm in his determination. Seeing Dhruva firm in his purpose, Narada was very happy. He blessed the boy and said, "Dhruva, verily Lord Narayana Himself is inspiring you. He then gave the boy Narayana Mantra in his ears, 'Om Namo Narayana!" As he heard the Mantra, there was a thrill in Dhruva and Concentrated on the Lord alone. In Madhuvana (forest) Dhruva carried severe austerities. He gave up food and devoted his body and mind in *Japa* throughout the day. Lord Narayana was very much pleased with Dhruva's words of thankfulness and gave him boon. There was great rejoicing throughout the kingdom for a number of days in honor of his return. In time Dhruva grew up to be a mighty king and ruled over a big kingdom for a long time. In Indian mythology he is dhruv tara or pole star. He never changes his position in the sky and all the other stars including the seven Maharishis go round and round him throughout the year. That is why he is called the Polar star.

Bhavna (feelings and intention) is also pre requisite to be the part of God's blessings. The fact can be traced from the Sikh history where Guru Amardas Sahib, the third Guru of Sikhs adopted Angad Dev Ji as his spiritual guide (Guru). He used to rise early in the morning, bring water from the Bias River for

Guru's bath, wash Guru ji clothes and fetch wood from the forest for the making up of the Guru Ka Langar. He was so dedicated to serving his Guru that he lost in his commitment that he was considered as an old man who had no interest in worldly affairs and was generally forsaken. However his sheer commitment to Sikh principles, dedication and service lead Guru Angad Sahib appointed Guru Amardas Sahib as Third Guru Nanak at the age of 73. This was a result of his services and devotion to Guru Angad Sahib and his teachings.

A Guru takes care of the fact that how much knowledge he has to give to his disciples because not everyone has the capacity to retain the knowledge, as excessive knowledge can lead to insanity.

A story will suffice the above mentioned fact:

Once there was a king of Kauru lineage. He was the bhakt of Lord Shiva. In the search of the unknown he reached Uttarkashi there he met a Brahman who asked him, "O king why are you wandering forsaken your kingdom when you can actually enjoy and partake in the best of the world?"

The king replied, "I do not know why I am wandering?"

The king said, "I am looking for a person who can answer to my queries"

The sage came in his real form, Guru Dattatreya and the king identified him as the person from ancient time who had read the scriptures which give enough knowledge to identify deity. He was giving the test to the king to know how determined he is on his path.

Guru Duttatreya said, "Ok so you are in search of a Guru or teacher ?

King replied, "Yes you are right, I am in search of a Guru."

King asked a question to Guru Dattatreya, "But you do not have any Guru so where did you get all your answers?"

Dattatreya answered, "I have many Gurus like Fire, water, wood, honeybee, maiden, a courtesan and many more. I can tell about my experiences and learnings from these" Then Guru Dattatreya started explaining to him. Guru Duttatrey made the king realize the intellectual aspect of the Yogi and how one can enhance his knowledge by just observing the people and the nature around him. The knowledge is just in front of us, it is the intellect of the person that determines and analyses. One should never belittle the presence of others as Guru Duttatrey recognized the Guru in all the people and the elements around him. In other words the book of wisdom is in us we just need to realize. It is the thought process of the person that extracts wisdom from the things around him. The knowledge is not confined to books.

The intervention of divine force is always needed in order to materialize the acquired knowledge. There is an indispensable role of god in making a person higher in stature both in thoughts as well as in actions. The King of wisdom and justice, Vikramaditya, after whose name the Samvat (calendar) started, also gathered all the wisdom by the intervention of God. God made him an able judge and the greatest emperor ever lived upon this earth.

The story goes like this:

King Vikramaditya went into a jungle for hunting. There he saw a deer and with all his skills he shot an arrow towards him, the arrow struck the innocent deer and he started crying out the name of god. God heard it and sent one of his disciples a great Guru of a certain sect to ascertain the situation. The Guru disguised a sage and went to Vikramaditya and said, " the deer who is crying out of the pain belongs to me as he has been calling the name of God and I being his servant now would give shelter to him."

Vikramaditya reacted and said, "As I have shot him the arrow therefore the prey belongs to me."

The deer died while their conversation, so sage challenged the king that if he would give life to him the deer will belong to the king.

The king said, "I cannot do this, but if you can then I would give the deer to you." The brahman with all his faith and tapasya gave life to the deer.

The king got astonished at that and said, "O sage I think you are not a hermit but someone else I beseech you to please disclose your identity."

On seeing the king's repentance on his actions and the obeisance towards him the sage disclosed his identity and said, "I am Guru Gorakh and have been sent by Lord Shiva."

The king became his disciple and started serving him. After some years the Guru Gorakh said to the king, "No doubt you are paying your sincere services to me but O king God has chosen you for some other things as you have served me like a humble disciple I am giving you a seat where your decisions will never go wrong and you shall always remain in the hearts of being for your wisdom, and will be known for your justice."

He also gave him a boon that from now onwards the Samvat (calendar) will be named after you. Having taken all the knowledge from the Guru and blessings the king went back to his kingdom to serve his people and country.

From the story above it is very clear that God's intervention is always there to make a person respectable in the society without his intervention and blessings even the knowledge gathered by hermit over the years cannot be of any use. One's humbleness and true to one's aim, that is the task that has been assigned by God, the very reason for our presence on this earth should be fulfilled fruitfully.

Whatever we do in the service of God, we all get the due course of it. There is nothing which remains due. Sometimes Guru gives his disciple beforehand, when the person thinks of offering something to almighty in any kind. Therefore we should make it a habit or a point not to blow our trumpets whenever we do something in the service of the Almighty. Moreover when we become calculative in giving our share in the service of God, the vice surfaces in the form of daan (charity) dosha (vice). It is the greatest dosha and when realize should be rooted out at the earliest possible.

One should not talk about others' negatives or doshas in others character because it leads to initialization of the said doshas in their disposition. Moreover the back biting of others lead to debiting of our good karmas and we invite avagunna (vices) in our actions and thoughts. Guru Nanak Dev ji has said in Japu ji Sahib that:

Kar Nindak Sar Kare Bhaar, Nanak Neech Kahe Vichaar (back biting increase our vices and it is the most defaming act committed by the person)

Love is the powerful medium to get closer to God. It is the miracle of love and that too unconditional to be the humble servant of God. In the shelter of true love one can achieve extraordinary things and blessings. We have read a lot of love stories in the history of our culture. It has always given the additional meaning, that a person in pursuit of God when takes the path of love, even God raises his stature to a great extent that people start worshipping them as the Messenger of Love.

Heer was an extremely beautiful woman, born into a wealthy family of the Sayyal clan in Jhang, Punjab. Ranjha, the first name was Dheedo of the Ranjha clan, was the youngest of four brothers and lives in the village 'Takht Hazara at the bank of the river Chenab. After a quarrel with his brothers over land, Ranjha left home, it is said that Ranjha left his home because his brothers' wives refused to give him food. Eventually he arrived in Heer's village and fell in love with her. Heer offered Ranjha a job as caretaker of her father's cattle. She became mesmerised by the way Ranjha played his flute and eventually fell in love with him. They used to meet each other secretly for many years until they were caught by Heer's jealous uncle, Kaido, and her parents Chuchak and Malki. Heer was forced by her family and the family priest to marry another man called Saida Khera.

Ranjha was heartbroken. He wandered the countryside alone, until eventually he met a 'jogi' (ascetic). After meeting Baba Gorakhnath the founder of the "Kanphata"(pierced ear) sect of jogis, at 'Tilla Jogian (the 'Hill of Ascetics) Ranjha becomes a jogi himself, piercing his ears and renouncing the material world. Reciting the name of the Lord, "Alakh Niranjan" he wandered all over the Punjab, eventually finding the village where Heer lived.

However, on the wedding day, Heer's jealous uncle Kaido poisons her food so that the wedding could not take place. Hearing this news, Ranjha rushes to aid Heer, but he becomes too late, as she had already eaten the poison and died. Brokenhearted once again, Ranjha takes the poisoned Laddu (sweet) which Heer had eaten and died by her side.

The Love of Heer-Ranjha made their stature so unique that people started worshiping them after his death. When he was alive he became the disciple of the Guru of the high order Guru Gorakhnath. It was due to his pure love for Heer and his unflinching faith in his love for which the journey he undertook in order to be with the Heer; whom he loved from the very core of his heart. The Almighty had to give him his due because when love attains the stature of sainthood.

The story of Heer and Ranjha has a deeper connotation - the relentless quest of man (humans) for God. Heer and Ranjha are buried in Heer's hometown, Jhang. It has become a place of worship.

In another extraordinary example of true love and devotion, there is always a place of a sufi saint Bulleh Shah. They demonstrate how different practices of Islam materialised unique notions of caste, influenced not just by Brahmanical values, but also the divisions of *biradaris* (clans) and genealogy. What's more, it's a story filled with literary genius, written in a language of love and longing that is seamless with spirituality. This is a story we must be told. Shah Inayat Qadiri was a *Shaikh* (spiritual teacher) to many in the Punjab region presently located in Pakistan. At that time, Bulleh Shah, an *Ashraf Syedi* (considered "upper" caste), was looking for a teacher. On hearing about Shah Inayat, he decided to meet him. After his meeting Bulleh Shah decided to become his disciple. Shah Inayat came from a lower caste. When Bulleh Shah's family had heard about this the family got very angry.

There are many verses of Shah Inayat and Bulleh Shah which describe the unique relationship of a Guru and Shishya and its stature. Later Bulleh Shah became a famous sufi saint.

Every individual spiritual journey is different and his path is also different. One cannot toe the same path as trodden by other individual to reach the final goal of our lives i.e. Almighty. We will all come across such kind of dilemmas and examinations but with sheer dint of faith and the trust in our Almighty and the guidance of the Guru we can pass all the possible hurdles.

I have tried to explain different approaches of humans and various sages to undertake spiritual development. These are different roots just to enhance the eternal energy or Kundalini energy. The stories do tell about the spiritual attainments and the idea is clear that the Yogic processes should not be limited to just the physical asanas and activities but to the development of a subtle body to reach a more conscious state. But the idea was also to establish the importance of a mentor or guide. Whatever may be the path, the goal is to develop eternal energy or KUNDALINI ENERGY to achieve the higher state of human consciousness.

CHAPTER 2

Spiritual Practices And Human Body

There are numerous practices of yoga or spiritualism that differ across religions and belief systems, it can be described by finding meaning and purpose in life. Even one system may have many different subtypes. Religion and spirituality are not very often understood in the same way, though they often overlap. Spirituality has a much broader understanding of an individual's connection with the transcendent aspects of life. Seeking a meaningful connection with something bigger than yourself can result in increased positive emotions. Transcendent moments are filled with many interrelated things, like most aspects of wellbeing. Self transcendent emotions are linked to increased spirituality.

If we want to understand the spiritual aspects of a human body then we should enquire into a physical body and physiology and moreover we should properly understand the need of our spiritual body. It is also important that we understand our capabilities to explore more spiritual energies, which are residing well within our body. The idea is to attain a more conscious state by doing yogic and meditative practices. There are certain common facets like *Chidakasha, Samadhi state, Turiya state,* state of consciousness which find broad applications in almost all spiritual practices but may have different names in the pursuit of the supreme or parbrahma.

Chidakasha is a Sanskrit term that means 'space of consciousness' or 'inner space'. The term comes from the Sanskrit roots, 'chit' meaning 'consciousness' and 'akasha' meaning 'ether', 'field' or ' space'. Chidakasha meditation or ' dharna', is concentration on this 'inner space of consciousness'. It is also associated with the 'ajna chakra', the 'guru chakra', positioned in the stomata behind the center head of the forehead. Yoga Vasishta speaks about the 'bhutakasha' (dealing with gross matter), 'chitakasha' (dealing with mental concepts) and ' chidakasha' (dealing with atman).

Chidakasha is the field of the mind which invokes a deeper enquiry because there is still the duality of the 'seer' and the 'seen'. This duality ceases to exist in 'Chidakasha' which is the field of *Pure Consciousness*. Chidakasha also means the 'ether of consciousness' and the space behind the forehead which is the seat of visualisation that links man with the conscious, subconscious, superconscious and also the object of meditation or ' ishta deva'.

'Turiya' in Sanskrit means three, the combination of three. Turiya pervades the three common states of consciousness, which are Waking state, Dreaming state and Dreamless deep sleep. In Advaita Vedanta, it is Jagrat, Swapna and Sushupti avastha respectively which are empirically experienced by human beings.

Advaita also tells the fourth state of 'turiya' which some describe as 'pure consciousness'. This is the state of liberation where one experiences the infinite 'ananda' and non- difference (Advaita). This state is measureless, neither cause nor effect, all pervading, without suffering, blissful, self - luminous and changeless. Turiya is also discussed in verse 7 of the Mandukya Upanishad.

In Kashmir Shaivism, they also speak about the fifth state of consciousness called 'Turiyatita' the state beyond Turiya. Turiyatita, also called the void or 'shunya', is the state where it attains liberation, otherwise known as 'jivanmukti' or ' moksha'. These types of texts are variously interpreted by different yogis and narrators, but wholesome the quest to search for the absolute truth or God is the main objective.

Parabrahman, the absolute God or the creator, is beyond science and logics. Spirituality deals with the matters related to God. One may ask how we can deal with the subject of God which is beyond logic? Such an unimaginable creator enters an imaginable item of the creation and gives some indications or experience to us. Therefore spirituality deals with such items of creation which are related to all universal known forms. The medium or material into which the God or energy forms entered is imaginable and can be discussed by logic. The medium has all its properties that draw properties for universal energy or God. Of course the properties of God are again certain selected properties of creation only. Such divine souls like Lord Siva exhibited the process of cloning. Such divine human incarnation exhibits both the properties of the natural human body as well as unimaginable divinity of God. When Lord Shiva created Veerabhadra from his hair all the anger of Lord Shiva entered Veerabhadra and we can say characteristics were transferred. Devotees worship Lord Veerabhadra as the exact incarnation of Lord Shiva. The present cloning about which you are astonished was already mentioned. People said that was unscientific and now say that it is scientific. The inquiry about the unknown with help of known tools is the search for the present scientific world

As per most of the yogic traditions the human body (sharir) has been differentiated in two major forms as physical body and subtle but there are also some references about different body types, like three sharirs: sthul sharira, linga sharira and karan sharira.

Sthul sharir or Gross body is physical body that is made up of the Panchmahabhutas, the five primordial elements, i.e., Akash (vacuum), Vayu (air), Agni (fire), Jal (water) and Prithvi (earth) and is subject to a sixfold change: birth, subsistence, growth, maturity, decay, and death. This is the dense physical body. Gross body is simply the vehicle of all the other Principles (bodies) during physical incarnation. Annamaya and part (physical manifestation) of Pranamaya Kosh reside in Gross (physical) body. Gross body needs material for sustenance which it gets from Annamaya and Pranamaya Kosha. Subtle or astral body (Linga Sharira) is where the mind and intellect. Manomaya and Gyanamaya Kosh and part of pranamaya kosha reside in Astral or Subtle body.

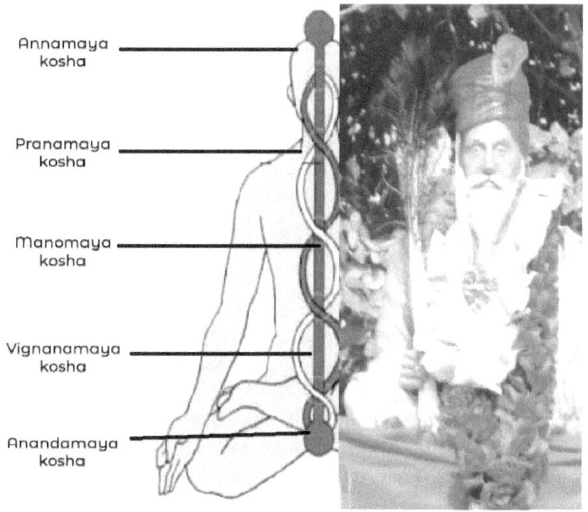

Fig. 2 Different types of Sharira

Linga Sharira contains pranamaya kosha, movement of the pranic force directing our physical and mental activities. This movement happens through nadis or channels, conductors of energy which are controlled by the six chakras.

Vital sheath is composed of vital energy which is essential for life. This sheath is responsible for our physiological functions namely breathing, digesting, metabolizing, circulation, endocrinal, neural, skeletal, muscular etc.

The Linga sharira or subtle body surrounds the Sthula Sharira (physical body) as an aura of energy. The Nadis (subtle energy channels) exist in this subtle medium through a fine merger into the physical medium. The vital body is just a raw form of physical body. Anandmaya Kosh resides in the Causal body

(Karana Sharira) of the sadhka and the Causal body needs some force from Anandmaya Kosh. Karana Sharira or Causal body is the cause for the gross and subtle bodies in the future birth of the soul and controls the formation and growth of the other two bodies, and determines every aspect of the next birth.

Karana Sharira is responsible for consciousness and is assosciated with the state of samadhi. It links individual consciousness with the collective consciousness. Experiences (samskaras) from our past lives are stored in the causal body; moreover the attachment and detachments are also linked to this sharir.

The Nadi system and chakra system are also major constituents in the spiritual form of the human body. NADI is a term for the channels through which, in traditional Indian medicine and spiritual knowledge, Nadi is a Sanskrit word which translates as 'tube,' 'channel,' or 'flow.' It is used to describe the network of channels which allow energy to travel through the body. NADI and CHAKRA systems determine the level of spirituality in any individual.

Prana the vital or life energy circulates through the body, but it can only do so if the pathways, or Nadis, are clear and free from blockages. Where the prana cannot flow freely, the mental, physical or emotional health of the person can be affected. There are 72000 nadis in YOGA SHASTRA but major three are:

1. Ida nadi: Also called the left channel, this starts in the root chakra (muladhara). It flows to the left, in and out of the other chakras up the spine, and ends up in the left nostril. It represents mental energy.

2. Pingala nadi. Also called the right channel, this starts in the same place - the root chakra - but instead flows to the right, up

the spine and ending at the right nostril. It is the origin of life force.

3 Sushumna nadi: Also called the central channel, this runs straight up the spine, through all of the chakras. Starting just below the root chakra, it heads right up to the crown chakra - the sahasrara. It is the nadi of spiritual awareness.

IT'S IMPORTANT THAT THE ENERGY FLOW IN BALANCED MANNER FOR THE SADHKA OTHERWISE SOME COMPLICATED NEUROPSYCHIATRIC PROBLEMS MAY ARISE. Many sadhka face hormonal changes or psychosomatic disorders also if the proper balance of energy flow is not established during sadhna.

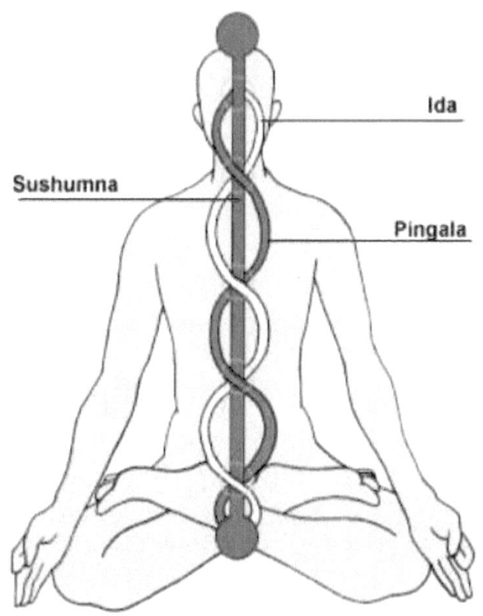

Fig. 3 Three major Nadis of human body

Chakras are commonly referred to as 'Energy Centres' Chakras are where people can exchange. In Indian tradition, there are seven Chakras (Sanskrit:wheel) inside the human body and they represent centers of energy along the spine.

There are a total 114 chakras in the human body and through these chakras, the energies flow. However, the seven main chakra points are more popular among yoga practitioners, and each of these seven chakras has its own distinct quality. Our energetic anatomy is made up of the Following structures, chakras, nadis aura, tantrika tantra, etc. Like the physical body we have, Chakras are the 'organs' of the energetic anatomy.

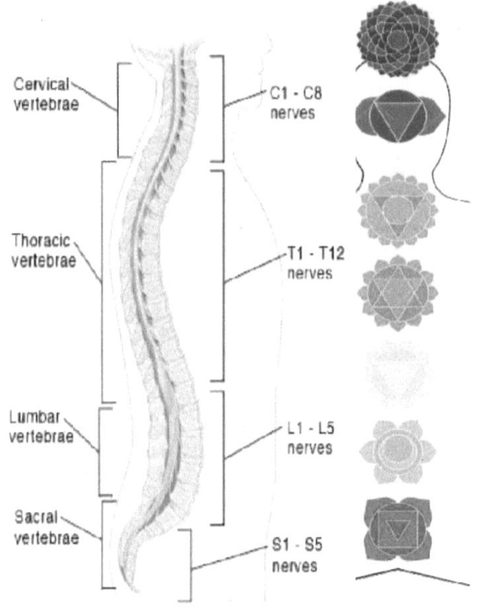

Fig. 4. Location of different chakras along spinal cord

Consciousness is closely related to the seven steps (related to chakras) of an individual's spirituality. If the Chakra system is in harmony, the Aura will be wider and has pleasant effects on the person. If not, the human body cannot function properly, which will lead to a series of problems.Hence, the Aura should be free from negative energies. For balancing the Aura's health and Chakras, regular practicing of yoga, Meditation, is a must, which will also enhance the healthy spirit and personality of an individual.

Chakrodaya (Rising of chakras) literally means rising of chakras. Rising of chakras is just like rising of your energy or light source. Chakras are part of Kundalini energy and they serve as energy centres of the human body. But many negative notions pose hindrance in energy flow in these chakras so it is important to do healing and proper cleansing of the chakras before going ahead with the rising or rising of Kundalini energy.These factors include fear, ego,internal negative thoughts, fear and various other factors which tend to give us negativities. These types of factors generally create confusion and health issues.So we need to understand that proper cleansing and meditative practices are to be followed.

HUMAN body consists of five elements. The 'Fire' element is very important. The fire element which is present inside our body can be invoked with regular practice of pranayama and specific yogic kriyas. We can go ahead with chakra sadhana and achieve our psychological as well as spiritual goals. Moreover, the efficiency of human body increases many times.

For *Chakrodaya* and *Kundalini awakening* there are various methods by which we can go ahead with this practice but this is in fact individualistic approaches needed rather than being generalized for all. Human body tends to respond differently from individual to individual to any energy changes or vibrations supplied by yogic kriyas so we need to analyze our capacity and ability to respond to those vibrations.

Different methodologies can be applied for the Kundalini awakening including like Laya yoga, Bhakti Yog, Tantra Yoga, Mantra Yoga and Shaktipat kriya can also be applied, moreover we can also apply combination of different types of methodologies to have more fruitful results but this combination and suitable Cocktail of these methodologies should be carefully handled and it becomes responsibility of mentor to diagnose the individual's capabilities and suitability of the methodology.

LAYA YOGA is any musical or dance combinations which has been referred in our text as like, these are very useful instrument to bring our body in rhythmic form and apart from your entertainment and all the things these are also used to get connected with supreme in the form of any devotional songs, music or dance forms.

In MANTRA and DHYANA YOGA different mantras like pranav manta, gayatri mantra, isht mantra are important, Gurumantra has supreme role. With the help of mantra chanting, a sadhka can improve concentration. A concentrated mind is a useful asset for the meditations and further yogic practices. The meditation on the devine forces is only possible with the help of a well focussed mind only.

BHAKTI YOG , during the medieval period many saints like Guru Nanak Kabir, Sant Ravidas Saint Namdev and various Sufi saint, propounded the idea of bhakti and pure devotion for the supreme this kind of devotion is basically the submission of a human body to the deity or any supreme energy so that we get our energy awakened. The path of devotion seems to be easy. Some people call this as Sahaja Yoga, but to be firm in one's devotion is also a tough job.

TANTRA YOGA there are various kriyas which has been referred for Kundalini awakening these may include some tantra practices which are very common in Himalayan and sub Himalayan region this type of practices.Different types of Shaktipats and telekinetic energy practice can also be used for Kundalini awakening and thus the the connection with the divine can be established.

KARMA YOGA, every aspect of nature is indulged in some or the other work. All Panchbhuta are collectively in harmony to perform some work. As a human body we are always doing work actively or passively. We cannot renounce work or Karma thus the world is called the Karma Bhoomi (place of work). Karma yoga can be a path for self realisation and thus experiencing the divine inside. As Gita says "Work without Expectations" certainly this is worship.

The routine practices are to be supplemented with Achar and Vichar, i.e. behavior and thoughts. Self-examination is vital on the path of spirituality as it should be the consistent effort on part of the trainee to get in control of his vices and should not get attached to his likeable virtues because it brings self-praise and ego in the psyche of the trainee. The feeling of competition amongst the disciples to be liked the most by the Guru brings a lot many vices in the character of the person. His behavior and the very chit (nature) concentrates more on the activities of other disciples and forgets his own desired self hence invites degeneration on his spiritual path. The development cannot happen in the presence of feeling of jealousy and the feeling of possessiveness hampers the growth of a disciple.

Knowledge cannot be put in a container. It is limitless; it is beyond the life of a person on this earth. Little knowledge is a dangerous thing, the main monster in the path of spirituality is the comparison, and ego of knowledge, copying others to instill the same values, the superior feelings, the feeling of equality with your Guru etc. are the gateways to spiritual degeneration.

Karmas should be done to perfect one's character, Karma is a Sanskrit word springing from the root "Kri" - "to do" or "to make" or more simply, "action". When we talk about "Our Karma" we're talking about the actions performed in the past (including our past lives) that are the cause of what we are in our current life situation. This either becomes our Karmic Burden or Karmic Baggage or our Karmic Blessing depending on whether we have done positive or negative actions in the past.

Every action, either physical, emotional or mental, every movement occurring either on the plane of gross matter (Sthoolam) or on the astral planes (Sookshma), causes an emission of energy and lays the basis of future events.

The innumerable Karmic will undoubtedly produce, sooner or later, a positive or negative result according to the nature of the seed, if not in this life, then in some future one.

The Vedas say that whatever we are getting in the present life are ultimately the fruit of our karma. Karma should not be confused with Fate. Fate is the notion that man's life is pre planned for him by some external power, and he has no control over his destiny. Karma on the other hand, can be corrected. Because man is a Conscious Being and he can be aware of his Karma and thus strive to change the course of events, with the help of superior powers. Krishna instructs Arjuna on the Karma of three types. First, that is *Satvika*, the one done in the mode of goodness, Second, *Rajasi*, performed in the mode of passion and Third, *Tamasi* , the one done in the mode of ignorance. The person must perform his or duties as human beings so the positive karmas accumulate with the passage of time and form the suitable base to achieve the higher level spiritual planes.

CHAPTER 3

Hindrances in the path of spirituality

A spiritual mind has many aspirations in the path of self development but the path has many struggles and challenges also. A good traveler accepts these challenges to explore more of the inner strength. It is like a research project to work on. We need to constantly analyze the situations and work to get the suitable output and to tune our sadhna with the phases in spiritual life. The practitioner and the mentor should communicate and address the problems and design the Yogic Kriyas in a holistic manner. The practice must be undertaken seriously and with utmost patience. Consistency is also a major factor because the awakening of Kundalini is not a matter of a few days, months, it may take years or whole life span.Some factors like intellect, enthusiasm, proper knowledge, committment are very crucial and must be well understood.

Firstly, I will talk about the intellect or the mental set up of the human body.

From the point of view of mental alertness, a spiritual seeker should always be attentive in his actions and yogic routines. There should not be any space for carelessness when doing any yogic practice. Sadhka must be alert about his behavior, words and actions. A little carelessness on the part of Sadhka may lead to a downfall in the energy levels and the growth may be retarded. Therefore our intellect should be guided and the alertness should be constantly maintained towards the ideal path in spirituality.

The sadhka may have different choices for yogic practices as there are different yoga schools so a practitioner must be able to choose the suitable path for this the sadhka should have ability to discriminate. The capacity to discriminate is one of the most important functions of intellect so the practitioner can become an ideal sadhka. Those who possess the capacity to discriminate between good and bad have the possession is like a golden asset in the spiritual path. It helps in making the right and quick decisions at the appropriate time. The lack of discrimination reduces the decision making capabilities and ultimately harming the individual motives.

Our motives and action should always be guided by serious and alert thinking and a decision should not be impulsive. Only the stable mind can discriminate between right and wrong so brain should be trained with constant practice so that we can really e develop the power of of discrimination. We know the differences between the good and the bad but very often we fail to make the right choices. It is basically due to lack of affirmative thinking and somehow related to our personal greed, in other terms can be called a want of luxury and comfort. These qualities reduce the power of descrimination. Most of the people know Dharma but Don't practice. This is the root cause of us suffering and one of the major obstacle In the spiritual path.

Unless we strengthen our mind and intellect we cannot become a good traveler in the spiritual path. The capacity of the mind needs to develop the subtle truth as we move ahead and the learning must go on in a spontaneous manner. Further more, with the modernization humans are losing the power of creativity, original ideas and discrimination which is not a healthy sign.

If we talk about enthusiasm, it has been observed that when we start any new work or project the aspirant is little over enthusiastic to pursue the goal but with passage of time the level of enthusiasm decreases though its very important to keep the same passion for longer duration. Enthusiasm is a driving force that triggers us to take actions and pursue goals. It becomes a frustrating situation if we have a goal that we wish to accomplish but we cannot awaken enough aspiration and motivation to take action. Due to this, we become nonchalant, unhappy and prefer to stay in the same situation without making progress. Many reasons like Shyness, Lack of Belief, Lack of Self-esteem, Negative thinking and Negative self-talk play an important role in aggravating the situation. One must not blame other people and circumstances in this situation and we need to realize the origin of the problem. A person should try to learn how to overcome and disregard those reasons by becoming aware of them, accepting them and changing the programming of his mind. Instead of suffering, feeling passive and uncomfortable. it would be much better to produce enough motivation to take action and do things. One should stop dwelling on problems and difficulties and start focusing on finding solutions and achieving goals. The absence of proper knowledge is also a big hindrance, a sadhka must understand.

General lack of knowledge is caused by the lack of proper awareness and education. Proper education is not about 'uploading' data into our brains which we usually think of as Memory but it means enabling our brain to connect us to the real source of true knowledge. This has been properly defined in Chapter IV of Srimad Bhagwad Gita by Lord Krishna also. "There are numerous reasons for lack of self knowledge, these reasons need to be identified and rectification must be done"

All these can be overcome easily with determination and strong belief. One needs to shut the doors of the past and do everything step by step. Age is no parameter to know what one is capable of. Try different things and widen your horizons in everyday matters that fill our day. One must have the courage and faith that you will learn what you don't know.

If we have proper knowledge and education about the path to be followed then the commitment comes next. Commitment can be defined as a dedication or obligation that binds an individual to a particular person, cause or course of action. Commitments may be made willingly or unwillingly and a fear of commitment can affect an individual's life in various ways. Such people may spend a lot of time questioning the relationship. They create distance in the relationship. They don't act into the future and are generally distrustful of people. They may remain bound by their past.

One's fear of commitment can often be addressed and treated in therapy or spiritual healing by the mentor. A therapist can often help an individual uncover potential causes of commitment issues and explore ways to work through them. However, those can be overcome by removing egoism, enhancing our skill set and believing in ourselves.

A fully committed sadhaka is a better performer. If somehow the desired results are not achieved then we need to step back and analyze our performance otherwise we won't be able to develop the self- discipline and vision to get the results we want. In order to make ourselves accountable, we need to set Micro goals and list them wisely. Emphasizing our strengths, Improving our weakness and Valuing our time are some of the steps to become more accountable.

Prajalpa has been defined variously in our scriptures, just to evaluate the improper conduct of the sadhka. Prajalpa means useless talk. In one of the shloka some hindrances in bhakti have been referred as;

atyāhāraḥ prayāsaś ca prajalpo niyamāgrahaḥ

jana-saṅgaś ca laulyaṁ ca ṣaḍbhir bhaktir vinaśyati

One's devotional service is spoiled when he becomes too entangled in the following six activities: (1) eating more than necessary or collecting more wealth than required; (2)

overindulgence worldly things; (3) talking unnecessarily; (4) practicing the scriptural rules only for the sake of show off; (5) associating with worldly-minded persons (6) being greedy.

In 1898, Srila Bhaktivinoda Thakura wrote a short Bengali commentary for Srila Rupa Goswami's Upadesamrta naming the Piyusa Varsini (a shower of Nectar). Piyusa Varsini consists of 11 shlokas. The principle of accepting everything that is conducive to bhakti and abandoning all that is detrimental to bhakti.

The impulses of speech, the mind, anger, the tongue, the stomach and the genitals are six impulses arising out of contact of the senses with their objects. Whosoever is capable of enduring these impulses, is certainly fit to rule the world. The water of the Ganges can purify even if there are bubbles or mud found in the water. The bubbles and mud don't stand in the way of purification. The devotee is only meant for the good of the universe.

Bhaktivinoda Thakura has mentioned eight types of Prajalpas in Piyusa Varsini which are impediments to devotional service. Prajalpa means 'prattle' or ' gossip'.

Argument is a prajalpa that is adverse to devotional service. All arguments of the followers of Nyaya and Vaisesika are simply godless quarrels. Useless arguments arise from envy, pride, aversion or attachment to sense gratification, foolishness or pride.

When a jiva comes into this world, he does 'jana sangha' (association of non-- devotees) and the result is material greed. He indulges more in Worldly Talks. The tongue has two activities, eating and speaking. Since tongue and mind are connected, so if we speak about the Lord, our mind gets filled with remembrance of Him only. Similarly if we speak nonsense with tongue, then the mind too gets filled with nonsense and it vibrates useless things like Gossip.

Finding faults in others and speaking falsehoods also are considered Prajalpas.

Debates are useful only if they help people develop their conviction. Devotees should be careful about not wasting too much time debating topics on which they have no control.

Blasphemy is also forbidden for spiritual travelers. One should mentally offer respect to that person who even chants and whose hearts are totally devoid of profanity to others. Lord Krishna explains to Arjuna in Srimad Bhagavad Gita (Chapter IV, Shloka 40) that he who has neither the 'knowledge of Self' nor ' the intellectual readiness' to fully understand the true import of the scriptural words of learned masters, will certainly get ruined. On the other hand I believe much of the information we acquire is useless but because of the social standards which are there, whenever there is a discussion between some people, everybody basically wants to show off how 'aware' I am of current situations. So, there is a culture of ostentation in knowledge which is irrelevant if not harmful. Some bad habits and behaviors which exist in all human beings are just enemies in self development likewise in the material world enemies and friends coexist in the material world, we create them for ourselves and we do it with our own thoughts, feelings, actions, sometimes knowingly or sometimes unknowingly. We form relationships, build bonds, make attachments, establish connections, nurture friendships, make acquaintances and on the other hand we detach from people, relationships and experience distress and disconnect physically and mentally with the loved ones.

The attachment and then detachment very often lead to emotional fluctuations and lastly to distress. The way we see ourselves and others with some sort of interactions and define how the relationships will develop, grow mature, sustain, survive or get destroyed. This image of one self is in constant discussion with our own thoughts, which relates to others and we interact with others according to our thought process only.

Aham means 'I' but in the limited sense it is always used in context with others it is often referred to as short form of of arrogance or in Hindi with term it as a 'Ahamkar' when a simple expression of 'I am' or a Aham gradually leads to and forcing thoughts ideas believes and imposing I and aham to everyone else in around us it becomes a ahamkara (ego) or simply where there is no space for others and their thoughts. The arrogance ultimately leads to stress, suffering and priority destructive mind set showroom and pay in simple terms ego doesn't allow for joy and happiness anymore. In Mahabharat Arjun ego was the attachment to the body due to ignorance until he was taught the lesson of Geeta by Lord Krishna, He then decided to follow the path of Karma after understanding that the real true self is eternal and it does not perish. So it's better to understand the value of teachings of Satguru or the mentor. The ego in us goes on creating enemies among friends and well wishers and thereby valuable relationships are compromised bringing misery, pain and sorrow into our lives so better to disown ego at earliest.

It must also be anger is an extension of ego it is also an expression of sadness whenever you app with anger deep within in you will actually be feeling sad day for anger is an active form of sadness similarly sadness is a passive form of anger when you cannot express your anger you feel sad within this is an observation made by swiss psychoanalyst Carl Gustav.

If you can tear through the masks of pretense and false prestige with which you have to try to hide a negative emotion like sadness and arrive at an honest answer to the question you are well on the way but you need to do a lot of homework before you overcome pretence. You have to identify the problems and work on them. If there is an expression of sadness removing sadness will automatically remove anger but the operator question is how we remove sadness dancer would be by cultivating happiness. If you look within or look at life around you you will find several reasons to be sad but try to look for things to be happy and laugh about. There is practical significance to this so you examine your own behaviour in comparable contexts and gradually egoless behaviour can be achieved.

The main goal of human life is to grow mentally if one wishes to grow in spiritual life and to deal with this path in a manner. We call a boy or a girl mature when he or she is gross in age but very often we tend to neglect the fact that age does not really mean the growth in IQ or intellectual level. If we are neglecting the intellect of humans it surely means we are ignoring an essential part of the spiritual life, so utmost care should be given for the improvement of mental and emotional health. A child should be educated right from the beginning and the educational materials are to be supplemented with such content so as to boost character and mental health.

Good mental health will awaken logical thinking in humans and with this kind of awakened mind one will accept the wisdom provided by the Gurus, Seers and Shastra. If a spiritual seeker is not mentally healthy he or she will succumb to a variety of temptations and confusions in this state of mind one can draw many types of angles for a single point of view and very often become prey to our intellect also.

With the growth of mental health the restless and turbulent thoughts reduce thus forming the basis of a motivated spiritual life. A sadhaka with good intellect and mature mind breaks all barriers and accepts the whole world with love by overcoming his or her hindrances. The growth of intellect the sadhaka conquers all pitiful and selfish ideas slowly and steadily cultivating important characteristics of pure intellect and total development. Sincere efforts are needed for this course.

CHAPTER 4

Different Faiths But One Thought

The world's faithful account for 83% of the global population. Majority of the population is connected to religious sentiments sometimes with conflicting philosophies about god. There is nothing wrong in exalting and respecting any god or goddess by devotees as most of the time a practitioner feels a special type of bond with his God but the trouble is basically when the faith of different people becomes a tool of hatred. In most of the religions the god is placed in heaven and mostly this like the interiority.

In this particular chapter I want to interrelate ideas of different faiths. Although very often humans advocate the supremacy of their own faith. It's a hard fact that people fell into a well defined agenda to propagate faiths not as a faith of individuals. In many texts it appears that the Quran, Vedic, or literature of other faiths are conflicting in their perceptions; actually their essential principles are basically the same. The god is one but different literature may seem different there are so many points of similarities that may not be easily detected due to many problems which are prevailing around this in the present world there is need to realise that the goal is one submission to the supreme.

It is also obvious that the followers of the particular faith in the understanding of their own scripts. Differences are not due to the content of the holy book itself, differences exist because different kinds of thinkers have different spiritual conceptions and perceptions. Differences of opinion arise due to diversity of nature and experiences so different interpretations are manufactured by the people around the world.

In general people are motivated to get their personal belongings and personal thoughts, in this way different individual mentalities are displayed in terms of their religious faith. One may be attached to any particular mistaken concept or maybe rejecting that another but it is having the same basic principle. So the defect is not to be found in religious literature but the credit to be given to the understanding and misrepresentation of the things. Now let us discuss the origin and basic conception of the five major faiths of the globe.

Hinduism and sanatana yoga systems :

Most scholars believe Hinduism started somewhere between 2300 B.C. and 1500 B.C. in the Indus Valley, near modern-day Pakistan. But many Hindus argue that their faith is timeless and has always existed.

Unlike other religions, Hinduism has no one founder but is instead a fusion of various beliefs. Around 1500 B.C., the Indo-Aryan people migrated to the Indus Valley, and their language and culture blended with that of the indigenous people living in the region. There are some debates over who influenced who more during this time. The period when the Vedas were composed became known as the "Vedic Period".Historians have different views on the time frame. Rituals, such as sacrifices and chanting, were common in the Vedic Period. The Epic, Puranic and Classic Periods took place between 500 B.C. and 500 A.D. Hindus began to emphasize the worship of deities, especially Vishnu, Shiva and Devi.It was the religion of an ancient people known as the Aryans ("noble people") whose philosophy, religion, and customs are recorded in their sacred texts known as the Vedas. These texts were initially handed over to students only orally . It was not until much later that they were actually written down. Archeological evidence from various civilizations of northwestern India show that Hinduism as the world's oldest living religion. Today, worldwide, over one billion people profess Hinduism and with time its growth has been tremendous. The fundamental teachings of Hinduism, which form the foundation of all its different sects, are contained in the concluding portion of the Vedas, and are therefore known as the Vedanta (the "end or concluding portion of the Vedas") also known as the Upanishads.

The fundamental teaching of Hinduism, or Vedanta, is that a human being's basic nature is not confined to the body or the mind but beyond both of these is the spirit or God within the soul. This spirit is within us and also within everything we see. All beings and all things are really, in their deepest essence, this pure or divine spirit, full of peace, full of joy and wisdom, ever united with God. This is not just theory, but it can actually be experienced. Anyone who takes the trouble to undergo the necessary training to purify and refine the mind and soul. This wholesome practice is yoga ("union"- union of the individual self with this inner spirit).

Yoga being the blood of Hinduism in almost all sects. Yoga is a practical aspect of the science of consciousness; it aims at the direct knowledge of consciousness and the actions of consciousness. The principle of yoga is the cultivation of a cognitive state of mind called Samadhi or putting together concentration integration with all efforts from mind, body and soul. It is also different from the waking state because it is free from distractions of all the worldly affairs. The attainment of Samadhi can be termed as a tranquil and sedative state of mind which is away from any subjectivity. Yoga is a long consistent and regular withdrawal to attain ever higher levels of consciousness since detachment and loneliness of the mind is the prerequisite for yogic kriyas, so yoga should not be defined in terms of physical exercises alone. On the other hand yoga is based on nature and natural principles. Mother nature is given utmost respect. Yogic system and Sanatan paddhati the God has been explained as a thing to be known by introspective nature only. The journey within the sadhaka needs to be prominent enough to realise the truth. The paths or approaches may be different but we are to reach the same destination.

Shiva and Shakti concept is the base of main yogic practices and schools in most of the Santan yoga paddhati. Here shakti is respected as mother nature and mother of the whole universe. The same principle fits alike in Jainism, Buddhism, Taoism etc. Himalayan tantras do also explain the essence of Shiva Shakti in the development of human consciousness. Even though the Kundalini yoga and major spiritual practices are just to develop the internal energy so as to achieve oneness with the supreme. We need to discuss the religious facets more scientifically in reference to human psychology and behavioral aspects.

Yoga and spiritual practices are just to liberate from complicated thought processes and make the life simpler and mind more pure. It has been observed that education and learning brings more complicated thoughts so it is not good. If education makes the mind of a person burdened then we are making mistakes somewhere.

Christianity and related faiths

Christianity is one of the Ibrahim religion like Judaism and Islam. Judaism developed as the first major monotheistic religion. The history begins with the conversation between God and Abraham. The nation of Israel has its descendants and Arabs Nations. The origin of Christianity is most intimately connected with Judaism. It started as a small group and later differentiated itself from the time of Jesus Christ. The world was largely under the domination of Roman empire. It began to spread rapidly sooner it became the official religion of Roman empire. Originally a Christian is most intimately connected with other Abrahimik religion is it developed into a religion clearly distinct from Judaism several decades from the Jesus death after the death of Jesus Jerusalem became the headquarters of the apostle original 12 disciples.

Philosophy is "the love of wisdom." The Philosophy of Christianity is the love of Divine Wisdom and humanity. Religion started from the teachings of Jesus in the 1st century AD. Its sacred scripture is the Bible. There are two versions of the book, Old Testament and New Testament. Its principal tenets are that Jesus is the Son of God and Jesus died to redeem humankind. Christianity was originally a movement of Jews who accepted Jesus as the main prophet.

The followers of Jesus knew that Jesus was a reincarnation, but were still not sure about his identity and offered several suggestions. Jesus himself gave no direct reply to the speculations, but he does confirm the disciples' ideas indirectly by encouraging their inquiry: 'But who do you say I am?' There are also significant descriptions in the New Testament (Matthew 14:1-2; 16:13-14; Mark 6:14-16; Luke 9:7-9) of the conjectures of various people, including Herod, as to whose soul Jesus might represent the reincarnation of. So these types of thoughts are somewhat similar to Indian faiths of yoga and santana padhati.

Book "Jesus lived in India " by Holger Kersten also reveals a lot about the unknown life of jesus. There are many references that he lived the life of a yogi in the state of himalayas. Even in Nath Yoga Sampraday (sect) of Hinduism gives references about the Christ, as Isha Nath. As most of the sects the teachings are in the form of *Shruti and Smriti,* these can be heard in the form of ballads.

Here the points are clear that Christ used somewhat similar practices for spiritual attainments like other yogis.

judaism also Abrahamik religion and it is almost practiced in Jewish land of Israel. The Jewish sacred text is called the Tanakh, the text is quite similar to the Old Testament. but they're placed in a slightly different order. The Torah, the first five books of the Tanakh, outlines laws for Jews to follow. The various teachings of Judaism generally propound the idea of monotheism. One God, the creator of the world, has freely elected the Jewish people for a unique relationship with himself. This one and only God has been affirmed by Jews in a variety of ways throughout history.

The principal message of the *Torah* is the absolute unity of God, His creation of the world and his concern for it, and his everlasting love with the people of Israel. The Pentateuch (five sacred books) both embodies the heritage of the Jewish people retelling its history, setting forth its guiding precepts and foretelling destiny and carries universal messages of monotheism and social conduct. *Torah* is also the origin of some other traditions, among them the recognition of the Sabbath or the day judgment. Basic purpose of these texts is to praise God and his acts and stress on prayers. Prayer builds the relationship between God and human beings. When people pray, they spend time with God. Praying regularly enables a person to get better at building their relationship with God. After all, most things get better with practice. Jews believe that God will take action in response to prayer (Midrash Tehillim 4:3)

Much of Jewish religious observances are done at home. This includes daily prayers which are said three times each day, in the morning, the afternoon, and after sunset. Congregational prayers usually take place in a synagogue, a Jewish temple.

Prayers or prarthna (in hindi) are a part of bhakti yoga practices that have positive effects on human bodies and souls.

Prayers are also a form of yoga called Bhakti yoga, emotional connection or devotion is important with God. In the bhakti tradition, prayer encompasses mantra repetition and chanting. People who regularly practice yoga or do exercise and indulge in continuous prayers, which is a kind of meditation, are healthier and live a peaceful life. It gives them an inner strength to work more effectively. It has been a well established fact that practising yoga or exercise and the daily prayers unites the mind and the heart of the individual and people are able to perceive the situations more analytically and work positively. So the prayers in any form or language have beneficial effects on human beings.

Muslims:

Muslims consider the Quran, their holy book which was revealed to the Islamic prophet and messenger Muhammad by God. The word "Muslim" was taken from arabic meaning "submitter" (to God of Allah). Islam, major world religion by the Prophet in Arabia in the 7th century. Allah is viewed as the sole God and is creator, sustainer, and restorer of the world.

Muhammad tried to cultivate brotherhood and a bond of faith among the people of the region. In this idea the prophet was very successful. In 622 CE, when the Prophet migrated to Madina, his preaching was soon accepted, and the community state of Islam emerged. During this early period, Islam acquired its characteristic ethos as a religion uniting in itself both the spiritual and temporal aspects of life moreover soon the faith could develope a big impact on a large part of population. The vast variety of races and people embraced by Islam All segments of Muslim society, however, are bound by a common faith and a sense of belonging to a single community.

Shahadah is the confession of faith. The confession of faith is the fundamental expression of Islamic faith and the core of all Islamic law as told in Quran "There is no God but God and Muhammad is the messenger of God" (la illaha illa 'lah Muhammadun rasul 'llah). The shahadah is the first thing spoken to a newborn and the last thing whispered into the ears of the dead. Salat (prayer): five prayers every day. These ritual prayers must be performed in the direction of Mecca and there is definite protocol for this. The prayers are read from the Quran and must be chanted from memory in Arabiyya, or the classical Arabic of the Quran. Personal prayers, called dua in Arabic, can be made in one's own language. Ramadan: the fast of the month of Ramadan to purify the soul. During the month of Ramadan fasting is done by muslims and the severity of the fast varies. *Zakat* (alms-giving). The Qur'an does not admire accumulation of wealth as the Christian gospels do; in fact, Islam manifestly understands the material world as created for the enjoyment of humanity. However, one's duties to God involve distributing one's wealth to the less fortunate. This is instituted in Islamic law, the Shariah, which constrains everyone to give some percentage of their wealth to the poor in the form of taxes (if one's wealth is in money). Just as the fast of Ramadan purifies the believer through renouncing the world, the zakat purifies the believer by encouraging a charitable disposition and a lack of attachment to worldly belongings. *Hajj* (the pilgrimage to Mecca): Every believer must once in their life make a pilgrimage to the Kabah, the sacred shrine of Islam in Mecca. Islam shares certain parallels with both Judaism and Christianity. As explained above, the three major sectarian divisions among Muslims did not originate in doctrinal disagreements. Although certain doctrinal differences among them developed over time, these do not affect essential core beliefs, which are shared universally by Muslims.

The God of Quranic revelation is, like the God of the Hebrew Bible, or any other religious books, they all believe in the creator of the universe and the ultimate judge before whom all people will eventually be called to account at the end of time. These dual qualities of creator and judge help to explain why the Koran stresses both God's mercy and wrath.

All religions, whether it is Islam, Buddhism, or Christianity have their fascinating history that needed to be studied so that we can understand their internal dynamism.

Many local literature of the Asia subcontinent show the relationship between Muslims (mainly Sufis) and Nath Yogis. Sufi communities have significant number of yogic texts and practices dealing with Hatha Yoga. There has been a particularly pronounced interest in the techniques of breath control and practices related to *kundalini*.

The collection of vernacular poetry attributed to Gorakhnāth (dating perhaps from the 13th/14th century, although the oldest manuscript found dates from the 17th century), and called *Gorakhbani*, contains several verses alluding to the peculiar status of Nath Yogis as neither Hindu nor Muslim. So there are many examples to prove that religious faiths have many basic functionaries with common principles.

Buddhism

Siddhartha Gautama is also known as "The Buddha," or "Lord Budha". The Lord Buddha was born in 623 BC in Lumbini located in Nepal.

Although born as prince, he realized that conditioned experiences could not provide lasting happiness or protection from suffering. After a long spiritual search he went into deep meditation, where he realized the true nature of mind. He achieved the state of unconditional and lasting happiness i.e. the state of enlightenment, of buddhahood, the stable state of mind free from any worldly affairs. For the rest of his life, the Buddha taught anyone who asked how they could reach the same state of mental peace.

The basic doctrines of early Buddhism, which remain common to all Buddhism, include the four noble truths: existence is suffering (*dukhka*); suffering has a cause, namely craving and attachment (*trishna*); the state of cessation of suffering, is nirvana state. There is an eightfold path to achieve *nirvana* of right views, right resolve, right speech, right action, right livelihood, right effort, right mindfulness, and right concentration.

The central Buddhism is the teaching of non-self also referred as *anatman* which can be realised with constant meditation. The five basic moral precepts, undertaken by members of monastic life, are to refrain from taking life, stealing, acting unchastely, speaking falsely, and drinking intoxicants. Members of monastic orders also take five additional precepts: to refrain from eating at improper times, from viewing secular entertainments, from using garlands, perfumes, and other bodily adornments. Their lives are further regulated by a large number of rules known as the Pratimoksa. The monastic order (sangha) is venerated as one of the three jewels, along with the dharma, or religious teaching, and the Buddha.

Buddhism arose in northeastern India in a period of great social change and intense religious activity. At this time in India, there was much discontent with Hindu high-caste. In northwestern

India there were scholars who tried to create a more personal and spiritual religion. Buddhism defines itself as Buddha Dharma or the dharma of the enlightened ones, which is seen as a tradition transcending time or place. The system has similar basic approaches in yogic and spiritual practices. The himalayan tantra and yogic practices have many overlapping techniques for self development and kundalini awakening.

91

Buddha taught the lesson of desirelessness: be desireless. He would say desires lead to a state in which we are always seeking that which we do not have. We begin to feel unhappy and dissatisfied for as long as our desires are not fulfilled in this state we cannot truly enjoy what we really do have. Desires push us to focus on fulfillment and we spend a lot of energy trying to obtain them each day. If we do not have them fulfilled is another day of happiness and so we live in this state of discontent when we are content with what we have we are truly happy as long as we are intrigued with the fall fleshy outer world we will continue on the wheel of disappointment. It is not the object what we desire it is our minds tendency to always be in the state of It leads us into attachment to think of the word it detracts from the purpose of our life to bring about communion with God of course this is the only true and lasting happiness that is the only true and lasting happiness. Nothing is permanent. Ultimately we are to lose everything that is widely a regular process for birth or death, even people whom we love our not permanent because we must leave the world or they have to leave the world through physical death. Nothing and no one in the world is lasting only our soul and god is lasting. Overall solution if we devote a time to seeking that which is not permanent. We spend a lot of time in search of the things which satisfy us and fulfill our desire that the same amount of time can be devoted to bring about union with the supreme. This alone is the lasting game with this comes eternal peace and contentment.

The meditation practice most respected by Buddhistst was the practice used by the Buddha on the night of his enlightenment is that of anapanasati. Anāpānasati is the recollection of inbreathing and outbreathing, as it were, a universal meditation subject. It is recommended as a character correcting practice; it is one of the foremost samatha (calming) subjects and it is perhaps the most natural, if not the most spectacular of vipassana (insight) meditation subjects. The basic principles of these techniques are logically similar to Kundalini awakening techniques.

Sikhism:

Sikhism is mainly concentrated in the Punjab area of South Asia present both in India and Pakistan. The Sikh faith began around 1500 CE, when Guru Nanak began teaching a faith that was quite distinct from Hinduism and Islam but all of the sikh gurus are from Hindu background. At a time when people were lost in endless intellectual discussions about God and self. Everyone was going and believing themselves to be right. Then a simple saint of great wisdom came by giving a call that the divine cannot be reduced to thoughts even by thinking many times. His teaching continued to be relevant to the world. Guru Nanak Dev had a unique place where he put forth the essence of all scriptures in the simplest words that people could understand and absorb. The first Guru of Sikhs would say you don't have to be scared of God after having a conversation with Siddhas. He said only a few people will be able to renounce the world but the highest knowledge is available for every human being irrespective of caste, class and circumstances, younger or old. Everyone qualifies to receive this knowledge from the experience and revolution. These teachings revolutionized the world. Guru Nanak Dev's contribution to Indian philosophy is unique, beautiful and timeless; it needs to be taught to every human being. Another beauty of teaching is the philosophy and practical living go hand in hand.

The teachings of Guru Nanak Dev show us the path of equality and social order. The dignity of women and gave special space to the woman as a creator. The uniqueness of his deep philosophical insights gave birth to the concept of the word 'secularism'. He was among the first who paid homage to the ideal of *Na ko Hindu, na Musalman* (there is no Hindu: there is no Musalman) and all are the creation of the Almighty. Leading an exemplary life, Guru Nanak presented a new vision of life.

The philosophy of Baba Nanak, from the very beginning, devised an in-built system for the cooperative provision of free food (langar), accommodation and security for the needy. All 10 human Gurus, Sikhs believe, were inhabited by a single spirit. Guru Gobind Singh ordered all sikh to worship *Guru Granth Sahib* ("The Granth as the Guru") as guru and furthermore there would be no guru. The final contribution of the Gurus came with Gobind Singh by forming the Khalsa. Sikhs practice virtues into their own character by reciting Gurbani, by listening to the singing of hymns from Gurbani, or by sitting in a quiet place and attentively thinking of God, forgetting all else.

This achievement or realization changes the thinking and behavior of such persons and instead of hurting others, they enjoy utilizing their life serving society. The belief of the oneness of humanity, and the insistence on working for the welfare of all people, whether Sikhs or not, at the cost of sacrificing one's life, is what sets Sikhism apart from religions. Guru Nanak Dev placed the motto of *"kirat karo, naam japo and vand chhako"* (work, worship and share) before his disciples. He stood for karma as the basis of dharma, and he transformed the idea of spiritualism into the ideology of social responsibility and social change. So Three Golden Rules which Sikhs follow are to remember God constantly, to earn an honest livelihood, and to share their earnings with everyone through charity.

Truth is the base of all religions but what is TRUTH?

God is a very form of truth, tapas and knowledge as the common notion of all religions . Spiritual energy cannot be seen without inner development. Most of the time we do not try to make the journey inward rather we show hatred for the other faiths, images or idols. Most of the faiths are different in some ways and the 'Truth' forms the base of all religious practices. But what exactly is truth and what is the definition of truth ?

The definition of the truth has various explanations in different religions and thus the approaches to search for the truth are different. The important angle is to concentrate on self realisation and introspection. Certainly and surely these basics are common for any faith. The aspirant searching for the truth slowly uncovers the sheaths of the human soul and then clears and polishes the consciousness. The conscious mind slowly leads to the union with the supreme.

Yoga is a Sanskrit word that comes from the root, "yuj" which means "to join together." Simply put, Yoga means "union." In many ways the term Yoga is similar to the English term, "communion." It refers to the state of union or communion with God, one's true Self, or Higher Power.

In Nath yoga, there is a concept of

"Nad, Bind and Yogi theen ka ek swabhav"

It means soul, body and devine, if these three are in union, then the sadhka or the aspirant becomes the Sidha.

One of the means of attaining yoga is worship of God as told in Ishwaraupnishad. It means love or devotion to God as the one centre of meditation. Our different races of humans are practicing different methodology for the same goal.

It is needless to say that every faith on this earth shows the path of righteousness and development of an individual as a good human being. For this we need to achieve the better lifestyle and a spiritually contented and peaceful life. This is the only method to stay happy and to maintain harmony amongst different faiths. When we talk about happiness the greater contentment is the need of the hour, this is precisely the reason why we should start a day by thanking the existence of the priceless gift of life from the supreme. When we look at the trees, mountains, rivers, the whole of nature outside of our home one thing in common is that all seem to be full of life in deep silent prayer. Researchers are now discovering that the sense of great gratefulness not only has a profound impact on our health but it also helps in reducing depression anxiety and treating sleep disorders.

Professor Alex wood and his team with Jeffrey Froh and Adam Geraghty In 2010 published a paper titled "Gratitude and well being: A review and theoretical integration" they concluded that gratitude is related to a variety of clinical relevant phenomena including psychopathological depression, adaptor personality characteristics positive social relationship and physical health particularly stress sleep etc. Religious texts are full of prayers and they all advocate that one should have a sense of gratitude towards the supreme so that we can always acknowledge his presence in our life and whole life becomes more positive and away from negativity.

In Bhagavad Gita Bhagwan Shri Krishna said to Arjun that you should surrender yourself to the Supreme so that you can receive the gift of peace, happiness and eternal abode. Sant Kabir gave this idea that "Tinka Kabhu na Nindiye" . Everything around us has some value. It should be respected equally. We need to acknowledge that everything the supreme is offering us has the potential to bring harmony and balance in life. Gratefulness is true union with the existence of the supreme. We should be grateful for breathing, for being heard and for having abundance of joy in life. Let this feeling of gratitude become an instant nature and slowly we will realise that all our complaints simply disappeared and leave us in the ocean of joyous celebration of bliss.

If we consider the present scenario of the world the inter-religion and intra-religion contradictions are on a very high scale. Individuals of the same religion and different religions may have different perspectives but the real problem arises when these differences of opinion become hatred.

Ethnicity is also a route cause of the conflicts and hatred as the religion or any faith system is determined only by birth and family lineage. The caste hierarchy in Hinduism is the worst example of the system.

If we want to really establish the human values in the faiths we need to propound the idea of Universal religion. Swami Vivekanand was the pioneer in the idea of universalisation in the modern time although this forms the base of Sanatan Padhati. The religion must not be limited to a particular geographical area, race or caste.

The idea of the universal religion cannot be pragmatic unless all humans on the planet accept the same level of consciousness. A good mental set up is required for this and thus only we can discover humanity. It must be understood by the human race that humanity is the privilege and heritage of life on earth.

On the other hand the ethnic groups have different cultural heritage and living priorities and these must be preserved. The cultural and spiritual values must be respected and given equal opportunities to flourish with mutual cooperation and harmony.

Faiths must coexist with peace.

CHAPTER 5

Concluding Remarks

Every faith does have the same idea based on these energy principles, but the problem arises due to different points of views and interests. The one race or the one group of people tends to have a sense of superiority over the others and it leads to a type of competitiveness amongst different communities. The problem is not the concept and understanding of the faith but the desire to prove the faith and desire to become more powerful. In this dilemma we very often fail to understand the concept of energy and biomechanics which is involved in our whole Kundalini Energy or Eternal Energy.

One who takes the path of faith and complete submission gets the reward to realise this infinite energy wherever you look and most probably the source is well inside your human body, a part of God the PARAM SHAKTI.

The fact is that one should know the concept of Kundalini Shakti which is prevailing inside our body in the form of ETERNAL ENERGY. There have been very western manifestations and scripts on the particular topic but I must say that when the Oneness of the Shiva and Shakti (Nadis) is really realised inside the human body the human body becomes a big source of life and spiritual attainments. The fact is that the human body should be realised more prevalently and realised in terms of a gift of the supreme. In this stage no psychological barriers pose hindrances in the growth of spiritual well being.

When the Kundalini Shakti in the form of ida, pingala and sushmna nadi originating from the base is realised then perfect solution and synchronization inside of the human body and the supreme can be attained. The human body becomes full of peace and grace from the supreme itself is a big celebration and joy in life.

There may be some psychological and physiological differences among different races and different types of human beings may be due to their faiths setups, may be due to their geographical differences or may be due to the cultural barriers. It must be most likely the human body, the body of *Homo sapiens* is more likely to behave one or the other way because in the same species that DNA as genetic material proteins and other physical activities are somewhat related and the principles of Kundalini energy will be equally applicable.

We need to put our thoughts in terms of Kundalini energy in all the human races present on the globe, so the concept of brotherhood is likely to be understood scientifically. Kundalini energy, a form of energy which is the internal energy in all human beings as propounded by the Sanatan Hindu paddhati. All human beings are just part of the Universal system. It should be understood very quickly and very prevalently so that we can really achieve the supreme stage which is the only goal of human life.

Hearing God's message is imperative when we enquire about subject matter beyond the purview of the limited senses and power of reasons. One cannot get perfect knowledge by direct perception or by the inductive method which is called just like presumptions. The process of direct perception is imperfect, for example. The Sun is not larger than a coin but in reality the sun is many times larger than the earth. Our human mind has its own limitation of perceptions of what we think. This knowledge is very often misleading in the context of broader aspects of religious faiths or the science of spirituality but a person who is on the top of these types of thoughts and is free from restricted thinking can really assume the greatness of *Supreme Energy* which is governing not even our body but every aspect of this universe.

Even in the present situation, spirituality is facing a lot of challenges. The true essence of eternal bliss and eternal consciousness is hard to find amongst present practitioners. Moreover if we consider the economy the lack of livelihood and starvation may not motivate one to seek higher pursuits in life. It is clear that spiritism cannot be practiced on an empty stomach. Though it is also important to understand that neither luxury not deprivation is conducive to one's spiritual development. We need to be in healthy condition so one should be able to think beyond oneself and thus the right to work and to achieve the basic subsistence income is necessary.

Apart from physical and imaginary hunger the third is spiritual hunger, the desire to be desireless that is beyond physical and mental place. This part will help us overcome mechanical nature and live life with utmost satisfaction. Living with equanimity and harmony with all beings surroundings and setting out society is the ideal living.

Present education does not awaken the mind, it feels it with the source of thoughts for the mind. It thus becomes an old burden and tired of feeding thoughts or feeding memories. It does not speak of our own internal intelligence. Memory is now a mechanical intelligence not consciousness. This concept is to be understood by an elaborated mind with the yogic practices. In the Spiritual path thoughts are not to be given to awaken from the worldly affairs. When thinking is awakened the mind is always young. Where the mind Is young the life is constant in constant phase of development and hence the spirituality will be more

If we summarise the thought process the spirituality should be free from outside imposition of any discipline. It should be dominated with intelligence generated from the conscious state of the individuals. If such intelligence becomes self discipline and furthermore if such self disciplined attitude is present towards life then he can achieve more goals in the path of spirituality.

There is a life force within your soul, seek that life. There is a gem in the mountain of your body, seek that mine. O traveller, if you are in search of that, don't look outside, look inside yourself and seek that.

-- Rumi

PRANAM !!! ADESH ADESH !!!

www.ingramcontent.com/pod-product-compliance
Lightning Source LLC
LaVergne TN
LVHW091119180726
843490LV00002B/850